# Faith on the Fire Line

*A brief history of the Fellowship of Christian Firefighters*

*International*

by

Members of

FCFInternational

Faith on the Fire Line—A brief history of the Fellowship of Christian Firefighters International

© 2012 The Fellowship of Christian Firefighters International
All scripture is quoted from the King James Version, KJV, unless stated otherwise.
ISBN-13: 9781482554687
ISBN-10: 1482554682

# Contents

| Ch. 1 | Early Days in Denver | 5 |
| Ch. 2 | Duncan Wilkie (1978-84) Spreading the Word | 17 |
| Ch. 3 | Bob Crum (1984-91) Vision-Driven Growth | 29 |
| Ch. 4 | Bill Guindon (1993-94)—Triumph through Transition | 43 |
| Ch. 5 | Gaius Reynolds (1995-2012)—Restoring the Reach | 55 |
| Ch. 6 | What's an "Encourager?" | 67 |
| Ch. 7 | Into All the World | 79 |
| Ch. 8 | Spreading the Word—Chapters Come to Life | 93 |
| Ch. 9 | The Darkest Day | 107 |
| Ch. 10 | Craig Duck—Facing Forward | 113 |

## Introduction

Written by current President/Missionary **Craig W. Duck**

History is important. By it, we shape our future. The fire service is full of history and tradition. We see this in the names we give to our departments, what we call our apparatus, and the names for the tools we use at emergencies. The heroic history of some departments has inspired the younger generation to do equal acts of bravery in their communities. Lost history for an organization can lead to a lack of direction and zeal. When the new generation fails to remember the struggles and sacrifices of past generations it is easy to settle for mediocrity. Joshua chapter four tells us a little about what God thinks of history; Joshua was commanded to set up twelve stones where they crossed the river Jordan. He was also instructed to teach their children the meaning of these stones. History is important.

Since 1977 the Fellowship of Christian Firefighters International has been ministering to first responders. Since that time FCFInternational has faced many struggles and difficulties. Great men and women of God, through prayer, would find out just how faithful God has been to the ministry. As you read through this historical account of FCFInternational you will learn the rich history that this ministry has had in the fire service. You will learn of how devoted past the past leaders of this ministry were to serving God. How God answered prayer and how the ministry took shape into what we see and experience today. You will discover how the early days shaped the ministry and how God used individuals to grow His ministry to first responders.

God brought about this history book in a special way. Wayne Detzler and I approached Gay and Sue Reynolds independently about writing a history book. Gay and Sue thought the idea was great and put the two of us together in order to begin the project. After several conversations with Wayne I soon discovered his love for writing and his God gifted ability to write. Wayne headed up the research and writing while Sue and I helped in organizing and proof reading the text. What a blessing to be able to work as a team in order to write the history of the Fellowship of Christian Firefighters International.

Our prayer is that this history book will inspire the next generation to do great things for God. I am convinced that most of us live far below our potential. Reading books like *Faith on the Fire Line* will inspire us to do more for God. As we read of the faith of those who have served before us we should naturally begin to pray for how God will use us in the fire service. There is a lot to be done for our Lord and Savior Jesus Christ, and the time is getting short. So what are you waiting for? Start reading and prepare to serve like those who started this ministry.

## Early Days in Denver

"Standing in line at the local Montgomery Ward department store we met by divine design," Bob Crum says as he recalls his first meeting with Duncan Wilkie. When Bob spotted Duncan and his wife, Bob joined them with a Christian greeting. This surprised Duncan, and they agreed to meet for some fellowship.

At home Duncan searched the Scriptures to find key verses, and he found one in Hebrews 10:24-25. "And let us consider how we may spur one another on toward love and good deeds. Let us not give up meeting together, as some are in the habit of doing, but let us encourage one another—and all the more as you see the Day approaching."

Fired up by the challenge, Bob and Duncan sent out invitations to all twenty-five firehouses in Denver inviting Christians to gather. They scheduled breakfast at a local restaurant which is always a favorite firefighter hang out. On that first morning, twenty-five firefighters showed up. The Fellowship of Christian Firefighters was born. A series of picnics and potluck suppers kept the vision and the fellowship going. Denver demonstrated itself to be a seedbed for the fellowship to grow.

## Three Guys—One Goal

Soon Bob and Duncan picked up a third Denver firefighter, John Barker. Together they would give shape and substance to the newborn fellowship. Each one brought special talents to the table.

**Duncan Wilkie** became president of the association. He joined the Denver Fire Department in 1955. Like Bob, Duncan came to faith in the early sixties, 1963 to be exact. He too was an engineer with the fire department, and in 1971 he was promoted to lieutenant. Duncan had been vice president of the local firefighters' union, and he played on several departmental teams, such as basketball and softball.

Early on he worked more than sixty-four hours a week, arriving home between 8:00 and 10:00 at night. The cost of this lifestyle was his marriage. "All I worked for was wiped out with one phone call to a divorce lawyer," Duncan recalls. He traveled the world and toured bars from Denver to Zermatt, Switzerland trying to forget his cares. "Life was like a beautiful soap bubble with all the colors of the rainbow," Duncan writes, "You reach out for it and POP, it's gone!"

His health suffered. An old basketball injury led to knee surgery. He hit on his therapist, but she refused to date him. She agreed to have coffee with him, if he would attend church with her.

The preacher "tore me up," Duncan remembers. He preached on the verse: "For what shall it profit a man, if he shall gain the whole world, and lose his own soul?" (Mark 8:36) Two things held Duncan back. First, God's offer was free; he couldn't buy it. Second, God's offer was love; he could not believe anyone loved him.

Finally on October 23, 1963 Duncan took the step of faith. He put his trust in the Lord Jesus Christ. Soon he enrolled in Bible school and prepared for the ministry. God brought Duncan on a circuitous route to redemption, but God was preparing him in time to meet Bob Crum and come up with the idea of a fellowship designed for firefighters. In 1972 Duncan was appointed to be a chaplain with the Denver Fire Department, as they recognized his value to firefighter support.

In the first edition of *The Encourager* Duncan gave an overview of the launch year when he wrote: "Praise God for His goodness to men! We are now blessed to share with one another what God is doing in our lives through *The Encourager*. In one short year, with direction and open doors by God's grace, we are an incorporated, non-profit, tax-deductible arm of encouragement for firefighters and related persons across the United States. God is doing a mighty work in the hearts of people and we want to share in this ministry." [1]

**Bob Crum** served as secretary of the Fellowship. He joined the Denver Fire Department in 1957. For the first few years of his career he lived without a personal relationship with the Lord. In 1962, Bob recalls, "The Lord turned my life around...and I accepted Jesus as my Savior." His first Sunday in church was in November 1963, a few days before the assassination of President John Kennedy in Dallas, Texas.

At the time of his conversion Bob was an engineer at Pumper #23 with the Denver Fire Department. He served at that department for thirty years, retiring in 1985.

Soon after his conversion Bob experienced a Billy Graham Crusade in Denver. At that time Bob was an usher, but the crusade left a deep imprint on his life. He became acquainted with the Navigators and dove into their "Studies in Christian Living." This grounded Bob in his Christian life and helped him to share his faith with others.

So Bob was primed by the Holy Spirit to meet Duncan Wilkie. The Lord had been challenging him to link up with other Christians in the Denver Fire Department, and that day at Montgomery Ward department store was planned in the counsels of heaven. Immediately the Lord bonded Bob to Duncan in a vision to network Christians within the Denver Fire Department.

Bob served as secretary and helped to launch *The Encourager* in 1978. The news sheet soon became a link between believers in the fire service. From the start Bob wrote a column titled, "From the Secretary." He launched it with this note: "What a joy it is for me to be able to share with you for the first time through *The Encourager*. Many of you have waited patiently for this first edition and prayed for us as we tried to get everything organized and operational." [2]

In his first column Bob reminded readers that they had claimed Hebrews 10:24-25 as the purpose of the group. The aim was simple: to encourage believers within the fire service as they live out their faith on the fire line.

**John Barker** filled out the leadership team as treasurer of the Fellowship. He joined the Denver Fire Department in 1966. Soon, however, he was drawn into the circle with Bob Crum and Duncan Wilkie. In his own words, John joined the department as a "Mucker," a truck driver before the days of power steering. He served in the Training Division for three years before becoming a company officer. Like most new officers he had a roaming assignment, serving in various firehouses. In the middle of his career he worked alongside Duncan Wilkie in the personnel office. John finished his service as a House Captain, in charge of one of Denver's fire stations.

John brought his gift for administration to the early Fellowship of Christian Firefighters leadership team. From the start he was one in heart and mind with Bob and Duncan, and together they would lead the Fellowship for several years. He introduced his son, Dan, to the fire service, and that son now serves as an engineer with the Denver Fire Department.

From the perspective of more than forty years, the plan of God becomes clear. God put Bob Crum, Duncan Wilkie, and John Barker together in the Denver Fire Department for a specific purpose: the founding of the Fellowship of Christian Firefighters. In the past four decades leaders and members have literally stood on the shoulders of these men of faith. They blazed the way for generations to come, and we do well to honor them. They have provided invaluable assistance in compiling this short history of the Fellowship of Christian Firefighters, and we are indebted to them for their kindness and patience in supplying information and inspiration to the project.

## Born by Prayer Alone

Prayer set the pace for the early life of the Fellowship of Christian Firefighters. Although they first met in 1970, the Fellowship of Christian Firefighters was not officially incorporated until 1977.

An early document raises yet another name as part of that pioneer band, who started the Fellowship. Duncan Wilkie had represented the group at the annual national fire convention Fire Department Instructor Conference (FDIC) in Memphis, Tennessee. On the return flight to Denver Duncan sat next to Ron Melot. Ron stated that during eighteen years in the fire service, he had never met another Christian firefighter. Ron encouraged Duncan to take the Fellowship into the national arena. This spurred Duncan, Bob, and John on to organize the Fellowship and reach out across the country and the world to other believers in the fire service.

Bob commented that this led to incorporation and a raft of legal and organizational details. Finally they launched the national organization at the national FDIC in Memphis. Membership dues were ten dollars, and thirty-five members signed up at that first conference. Later this conference relocated to Indianapolis, where it remains as one of the largest events of its kind.

The purpose of the Fellowship of Christian Firefighters was set out in nine major points; to glorify God in the Fire Service, find fellowship together for individual growth in the Christian life, serve the cause of Christ through the church of one's own choice, encourage those in the Fire Service in their Christian lives, bring all Christians in the Fire Service to a common goal of praying for the Fire Service and its members, share on an international basis through an Annual International Conference, have international contact with fellow Christian firefighters, care for widows—meeting spiritual as well as physical needs, and to place racks with tracts and Bibles in firehouses.

These purposes have shaped the growth and expansion of the Fellowship ever since they were formulated.

A very simple Statement of Faith supports the purposes of Fellowship of Christian Firefighters International (FCFI). We believe:

1. The Bible is the inspired Word of God, inerrant in the original writings and is the supreme and final authority for our life and faith. (2 Tim. 3:17-17; 1 Pet. 1:20-21)
2. There is one God eternally existing in three persons: the Father, the Son, and the Holy Spirit. (1 Cor. 8:6; Acts 1:2)
3. Our Lord Jesus Christ is the Son of God, conceived of the Holy Spirit, to Mary a virgin. He died on a cross, the shedding of his blood was the atonement for our sins. He was raised from the dead, ascended into heaven, where he is our advocate at the

Father's right hand. (Heb. 10:12; Luke 1:27, 35; 1 Cor. 15:3-4; John 14:2; 1 John 2:1; 1 Pet. 1:19)

4. That all persons are born with a sinful nature, thus separated from God. We know all those, who by faith believe in the Lord and accept him as personal Savior, are born again of the Holy Spirit. (Rom. 5:12; Eph. 2:8-9)

5. In the personal and positive return of Jesus for his church. (John 14:3)

6. In the spiritual unity of believers in our Lord Jesus Christ. (John 1:2; Eph. 4:3;

1 John 1:7)

It is noteworthy that founders crafted both the purpose statement and the statement of faith in such a way that believers of various denominations and affiliations could find a home in the Fellowship. In fact, very little notice is taken of the church background of the various members. They are one in the Lord serving the cause of Christ in the fire service.

John Barker recalls firefighters coming to the booths at conventions and standing in amazement that a Christian fellowship exists in the fire service. Very often, as John recalls, they would remark: "I didn't know there were any other Christians in the fire service." Then he added: "There is a need for an organization like this, praise God."

As a side note, John adds: "The response at the conventions was very surprising to me. I was amazed at the number of Christians in this macho profession. God knew what He was doing when He formed the FCFI!!!" [3]

The secret of success for the Fellowship was and remains simple. It is prayer. John and Bob met once a week for prayer. At first they did not pay attention to dates and times, because they did not think it was important. Only later did they realize that they were making history.

### Reaching the United States

Ron Melot urged Duncan and Bob to spread the Gospel message across the country. When the first edition of *The Encourager* was published this vision was taking shape. Bob Crum included letters from several local groups, early chapters of FCF.

From Pennsylvania a firefighter wrote: "The idea of such a fellowship in this area is challenging but I believe very possible as there are many of us who have accepted Christ as Savior and this could be just the way to bring us together." This shows how novel was the idea of FCF.

An Alaskan firefighter wrote: "Our group formed about a year and a half ago when we agreed in prayer for the safety of the city we protect." Then he added in amazement: "You should see how our fire statistics have dropped," since prayer began. They meet for lunch each week and spent the time in prayer for their city.

Cautiously the Alaskan correspondent added, "Our group may be too small for affiliation with a national organization." Duncan Wilkie hastened to insert this encouragement: "No group is too small, we allow individual memberships to our organization and then will pray with you for a local group and pass on names as the Lord sends them to us for forming local, city, metropolitan, or state charters as is best suited for each situation."

A long way from Alaska is the Gulf Coast of Louisiana. Correspondents from there agreed: "We do feel that there is a need in the Fire Service for a nationwide Fellowship of Christian Firefighters and especially local chapters." Beyond this ringing affirmation, the Louisiana firefighter dreamed a bit: "This would enable us to get to know committed Christian firefighters all over the state and would be a spiritual asset to all of us."

A firefighter representing Washington State wrote a letter to FCF headquarters in Denver. He reported on the second prayer breakfast. It met less than a month after the first one. Attendance doubled to six for the second event. Then he added: "I have been encouraged by God's work in our department during that time span. He has really done a new thing."

The Washington correspondent added that he served with a volunteer department. He had forged links with the chief of another department in that area. Beyond this the correspondent reached out to Portland, Oregon firefighters. Apparently six members signed up for a potential chapter in Portland.

In the second edition of *The Encourager* the first "Meet A Member" column appears. It is a personal testimony from Chief Kenneth Henry of Brandon, Florida. He was converted to Christ in

1973, and in 1978 he writes as a representative of the FCF chapter in central Florida.

When the next edition appeared, there was a "Meet A Member" column written by Fire Marshall Jim Dalton of Montgomery County, Maryland. This demonstrates a strong connection to the east coast for the Fellowship of Christian Firefighters.

Thanks to *The Encourager*, a chapter emerged in Minnesota. A group of firefighters had been gathering since 1976, and they were now gathering one day a week for prayer breakfast. They had met weekly for almost two years.

By 1978 Fellowship of Christian Firefighters was spreading like wild fire. Each edition of *The Encourager* brought news of FCF chapters emerging across the United States. The team of Duncan Wilkie, Bob Crum, and John Barker kept busy receiving reports of new chapters and corresponding with interested firefighters across the United States.

# Chapter

## Duncan Wilkie (1978-84) Spreading the Word.

"The membership is pushing upward to the nine hundred mark, praise God," Duncan Wilkie wrote in September-October 1980 issue of *The Encourager*. Then he added: "We have twenty chapters in the U.S.A. with more being in process at this time."[4]

Duncan graduated from Bible school with hopes of entering into a missionary ministry among the Jewish people. However, God had a different plan for him. He will serve as the first president of the fledgling Fellowship of Christian Firefighters.

<u>Casting a Vision</u>

In many ways Duncan's great gift was casting a vision, leading the organization upward and onward into bigger days. In the same article, he reminded readers that there were at that time 1.5 million firefighters in the United States. Duncan could foresee the day when FCF would have ten thousand members.

"Our goal is to place Bibles in firehouses around the world," he believed that firefighter Bibles would be printed in every major language of the world. One Dr. Marie Berg was already translating literature into German, and plans were underway to expand into Spanish and French. No one could have known how many Spanish-speaking firefighters would ultimately serve in the United States.

Continuing to cast vision, Duncan urged the members to pray for a massive ingathering of souls. "Five million souls for Jesus is another goal that we ask you to pray for also," his vision knew no limits.

On a local scale, the Denver chapter hosted a spaghetti dinner for firefighters and their families. More than 175 showed up for the dinner in Colorado Springs. A Christian football player from the Denver Broncos was the speaker and special music rounded out the evening. This high-impact event helped to publicize the growth of FCF in its own backyard.

Bob Crum presented his secretarial report in the spring 1980 issue of *The Encourager*. According to his calculations, there were 650 members in fourteen different chapters scattered across the country and around the world.[5] This showed considerable expansion during the first three years of the fellowship's existence. By May-June 1981 the number of chapters almost doubled to twenty-six. There was a definite growth spurt in the early years of Fellowship of Christian Firefighters International (FCFI). Thanks to the team of Duncan Wilkie, Bob Crum, and John Barker, correspondence seemed to thrive, as is indicated by numerous reports in *The Encourager*. This is remarkable when one considers that there was neither Internet nor email at that time. All correspondence was by letter, and many of them survive in the archives of FCFI.

## Reaching Out

Under the aggressive, itinerant ministry of Duncan Wilkie word spread like wildfire to firefighters across the country and around the world. In July 1979 FCFI was able to place a Bible in each dormitory room at the National Fire Academy. FCFI aimed to become for the fire service what Gideons were and are to the hotel business. One note indicated that three hundred Bibles were designated for the National Fire Academy, illustrating the size of this task.

Still spreading the word, Duncan Wilkie presented a plaque to Gen. Louis Giuffrida, training director of the Federal Emergency Management Agency (FEMA). A photo of this presentation is included in the October-December issue of *The Encourager*. The name and role of FCFI was starting to catch on within the first responder community across the country.

Enormous impetus to Bible placement came from a joint Presidential and Congressional Proclamation by Ronald Reagan declaring 1983 to be the Year of the Bible in the United States. This appears in a note accompanying a picture of the Chief of Lima Ohio Fire Department receiving Bibles from two of the chaplains. Such a high public acknowledgement of the Bible and its value spurred FCFI on to an even more aggressive program of placing Bibles in firehouses across the country and overseas.

In the spring 1983 edition of *The Encourager* a "Meet A Member" profile of Capt. John Barker, Denver Fire Department, appears. Capt. Barker was the original treasurer of FCFI, and he later assisted Duncan Wilkie in the personnel office of the Denver Fire Department. John traced his spiritual growth to working alongside Duncan Wilkie and Bob Crum in the original office of FCFI.[6]

During the summer of 1983 FCFI branched out even further by locating a second Family Camp in the Appalachian Mountains at Black Mountain, NC. This strengthened the position of the fellowship in the eastern United States as it served to draw into an orbit of influence for many firefighters from the eastern states.

While studying the early editions of *The Encourager*, one is amazed at the rapid growth and spread of FCFI. From earliest days this regular report tied together the chapters and members of the fellowship. Bob Crum edited it in the Denver office, and remarkably he was able to produce full editions despite the lack of electronic assistance. He excerpted letters and included them as chapter reports from both the U.S.A. and also from foreign countries, such as Canada and Australia.

### Power through Prayer

Early leaders knew well the absolute necessity of prayer. In the January-February 1980 edition of *The Encourager*, Duncan Wilkie called the fellowship to renewed prayer. In an article titled, "PRAYER—Format and Faith," he drew strong applications from the Lord's Prayer. He called it "the format for faith," and he asserted: "What this format for prayer given by Jesus tells me is: I am a worthy person. I am loved by God. I am forgiven. My needs are already met. I am kept and protected by my Heavenly Father." Notice the pointed practicality of Duncan Wilkie's exposition.

Then he moved on to challenge the members to pointed, practical, and powerful prayer for 1980. "I challenge you to trust the Lord for a special need or want in 1980." Then he added: "Allow Him to fulfill His promises from His Word in you." [7]

## Home and Family Building

Wilkie was also committed to illustrating his point by the lives of firefighters. He mentioned a young firefighter, whose wife had begun to cheat. The firefighter committed to Bible study and prayer. Later his wife became very ill, and her boyfriends all fled the scene. The firefighter devoted himself to caring for his wife in her illness, and as Duncan tells the story, twenty-five years later the firefighter and his wife are living for the Lord.

This very basic approach to the Christian life is one of the strengths of the FCFI community. Serving amid the heat and filth of the fire line, firefighters need to hear that God is right there with them. In order to strengthen firefighter families, FCFI emphasized family camps from the beginning. Both Duncan and John had experienced the stress and fracture that the fire service can cause to a marriage, so they were especially eager to build better marriages through family camps.

Special emphasis in *The Encourager* for May-June 1981 fell on the coming camp for families at Colorado's Snow Mountain Ranch. The chosen speaker was an outstanding young pastor and preacher, the Rev. Byron MacDonald. Pastor MacDonald had left his native Michigan to pursue theological studies in Denver, and there he came into a period of unusual blessing in his ministry. By 1981 he was listed in *Who's Who in America*.

In the summer edition of *The Encourager* a report highlighted the recent camp, reporting on its results. Several attendees wrote to thank FCFI for organizing the conference. Many mentioned that they found new friends in the fire service, and these friendships blossomed through correspondence since the conference. One summed it up, when he wrote: "I am back to work now and have shared with quite a few people the 'Conference in the Rockies.' It was well worth the trip." [8]

By 1983 the concept of a conference for families spread east to North Carolina. Beginning in that year a family conference came together at Black Mountain in the wooded hills of the Appalachians. The setting was markedly different from Colorado, but the plan was the same: to enrich fire service families and strengthen the bond between husbands and wives.

An interesting side effect of expanded ministry was the larger needs of the Fellowship. Thus in September 1980 the annual dues were increased from a very modest $10 per year to an equally modest $15. New members were charged $25 in dues for their first registration.

The financial viability of FCFI was demonstrated by John Barker's treasurer's report in 1982. During the previous year (1981) total income to the Fellowship was $28,855. For the same period expenditures were $23,931. The honesty of this report is only matched by the transparent integrity of the leadership team. They were completely honest with the members, so that each member could have a sense of ownership of the ministry.

As one peruses successive issues of *The Encourager*, one comes away with a sense that the leadership team of Duncan Wilkie, Bob Crum, and John Barker were thoroughly upright and devoted to the task before them.

Chapter Reports—At Home and Abroad

By the end of his presidential term, Duncan Wilkie and his team had seen remarkable increases in the number of chapters around the country and across the world. Each edition of *The Encourager* contains short reports from the field. The ability to collect, sort, and publish these reports is largely the work of Bob Crum as secretary. We must continually remind ourselves that this active correspondence existed long before the electronic age, and files of letters prove this point.

<u>Ontario, Canada</u>. In the January-February 1980 edition the trademark "Meet a Member" column featured Chief Larry T. R. Underhill of the North York Fire District in Ontario, Canada. He concludes by writing: "The Lord introduced me to the Fellowship of Christian Firefighters about a year ago." Then he added, "I am so thankful that God has raised up such an organization for such a time as this." [9]

Chief Underhill's report underscores the welcome that FCFI received in Canada, both in the eastern province of Ontario and also in the western provinces, such as Alberta. A later edition carried the picture of Bible presentation at the Ontario Fire College, a further demonstration of the activity of this Toronto area chapter. Additionally the Toronto chapter sent out teams of firefighters to bring testimonies in local churches. This is an early forerunner of the 911, Emergency Services, or First Responder Services.

<u>Washington, D.C.</u> Another "hot spot" of FCFI became the Washington, D.C. area. The Rockville, MD chapter placed Bibles in firehouses. The first woman featured in "Meet A Member" was Josephine Porter. She is identified as a Women's Auxiliary Member and Secretary of the Prince George's County Fellowship of Christian Firefighters. Her husband had been chief of a volunteer fire department, and Josephine wrote: "When our young children no longer demanded so much of my time and attention, I too succumbed to the 'siren call' and became involved" in many auxiliary committees. She emphasized the importance of praying for FCFI both in its local and its national and international ministry. [10]

A powerful testimony came from Frank Palumbo, retired New York firefighter and former secretary-treasurer of the International Association of Fire Fighters (IAFF). After faithfully serving the union Frank ran for president, and he lost the election. This plunged him into a period of joblessness. He was at the end of himself, when Ken Cox from the District of Columbia Fire Department reached out to him. Ken Cox was a union official in D.C. and a political supporter of Frank. As a result Frank became a believer in the Lord and his life was turned around. Amazingly, Frank came to believe that God caused him to lose the election, so that he would be "crowded to Christ," as someone put it. [11]

Another Washington, D.C. area department is the Laytonsville District VFD in Montgomery County, MD. From that department Chief James Snyder also added a column. Ironically the title, "Meet a Member," is not included in this particular issue.

<u>Emmitsburg, MD</u>. At the same time reference appears to the dedication of the Fallen Firefighters Memorial at the National Fire Academy in Emmitsburg, MD. When the memorial was dedicated, Duncan Wilkie represented FCFI and laid a wreath in remembrance. Duncan is pictured with the FCFI wreath, as it stands next to another wreath from President Ronald Reagan. At that time also an emblem of FCFI was hung in the dining hall of the National Fire Academy as one of the organizations dedicated to serve firefighters in the United States.

<u>California.</u> High profile presentations are matched by modest messages from lone firefighters or small groups. One such message comes from Modesto, CA. A firefighter at the Riverbank Army Ammo Plant recounts how he came to the Lord in May 1975: "He [Jesus] has changed my desires and attitudes about and toward other people as well as given me the wonderful gift of eternal life." He sees also that God has placed him in the fire service to win others. [12]

Michigan. From a firefighter comes a ringing endorsement of the Bible placement ministry of FCFI. He prays that the Bibles placed in firehouses, "will light the way for many a firefighter crawling on his belly through black, thick smoke." Then he adds, "For the Bible will generate his light from within and strengthen his courage." [13]

Australia. A photo in *The Encourager* portrays Bob Crum and Duncan Wilkie presenting a charter to Len Carter for the Menai District chapter of FCFI from Sydney, Australia. This constitutes the first such chapter in Australia and marks a step forward for the international advancement of FCFI.

Alaska. One of the earliest affiliates of FCFI was located in Alaska, and the correspondent reported on a regular basis. In 1980 he wrote:" He [the Lord] has also blessed us here over the past few years with an ever-increasing number of dedications and rededications among our own department." [14]

England. From England comes a report of cooperative effort with FCFI. Pete Slade writes about his attempts to connect with Christian firefighters in London, England. A year later FCFI sent materials for a display at the annual conference in England of the "Fire Services and Salvage Corps Christian Fellowship." Despite the quaint name, there is a common purpose with FCFI. (Just a brief editorial note might help. Across England there are many such fellowships linking Christians in various professions. It is a natural connection for FCFI.) [15]

<u>Wyoming</u>. A group of volunteer firefighters started a department within an honor farm, a penal institution. FCFI sent a shipment of Bibles and a box of *The Encourager* to them. This very practical outreach demonstrated the evangelistic thrust of FCFI during the presidency of Duncan Wilkie.

From the uppermost to the uttermost, FCFI was committed to send the gospel. In the early 1980s a series of tracts appeared, in which various members shared their personal testimony of faith in the Lord Jesus Christ. This added one more element to the evangelistic approach towards Christian firefighters.

# Chapter 3

## Bob Crum (1984-91) Vision-Driven Growth

Early in his presidency Bob Crum reminded the Fellowship of its vision statement: "To glorify God by encouraging, equipping, and challenging all Christian firefighters to make an impact for Christ through their individual and collective ministries in the fire service mission field worldwide." [16]

Then he unpacked this vision to explain that we seek a chapter in "every state of the United States, every province of Canada and every other country worldwide." For this reason he set the goal that every converted firefighter might be affiliated with a chapter of FCFI. To this end plans were laid for a Leadership Conference early in 1996.

Bob Crum is a man of audacious faith. He simply believes that there is nothing impossible for God, a principle as old as Abraham. Bob reminds us, "As a Christian firefighter you have been divinely placed in the fire service as an ambassador for the Lord."

It is this all-embracing vision that motivated Bob to unceasing effort and encouragement as he traveled from chapter to chapter, from one fire conference to another. He believed God wanted him to set goals, "without fear of failure." This bold approach to planning spurred on the organization from the earliest days in the 1970s until Bob's retirement in the early 1990s.

## Leading the Leaders

Bob Crum knew how to capture the hearts of leaders within the fire service. His early training at the hands of the Navigators had equipped him to identify potential leaders, train them, and send them off into their ministry.

Echoing Christian leaders who had gone before him, Bob embraced the truth that "it is always too soon to quit." In an early edition of *The Encourager* he wrote: "If your present position of service was given you by Christ, and He has not yet said, throw in the towel, don't quit! People given assignments by God should not lose heart." [17]

He set before FCFI fellow leaders a model of prayerful persistence. In support of this he introduced George Muller, who provided for 2,000 orphans in Bristol, England by prayer alone. Muller never asked any person for money. He only asked God, and God came through.

Introducing the Navigator pamphlet, "Seven Minutes With God," Bob urged leaders to spend time before the Lord in prayer. At one conference he taught FCFI leaders how to expand that time to one hour with God each day. Bob knew that the secret of spiritual success lie in consistent commitment to meet God every day.

When Thanksgiving rolled around in 1988, Bob used this to encourage an attitude of gratitude among the FCFI leaders. Then he added: "Thanksgiving should be a heartfelt response of all believers because of what the Lord has done." [18]

Bob led the eighth FCFI leadership conference at Glen Eyrie, the picturesque Navigator headquarters set in the mountains around Colorado Springs. Here he identified a young, Navigator-trained leader, Bill Guindon, and challenged Bill to become a roaming ambassador for FCFI.

Not only did Bob deepen the leadership of FCFI, he also reached out to other similar ministries. He built bridges to the Fire Service Christian Fellowship in England, especially to the strong ministry among the London Fire Brigade members. This ministry drew strength from its connection with the London City Mission and its intrepid band of "city missioners." Furthermore, Bob made friends with leaders of Firefighters for Christ in the United States, as well as Ed Stauffer's emerging Fellowship (later Federation) of Fire Chaplains.

For most of his presidency Bob worked alongside Pastor Byron MacDonald. The pastor's deep devotional writings occupied a major place in each edition of *The Encourager*. Pastor MacDonald also became a speaker at various FCFI conferences in the Colorado Mountains.

By 1991 Bob had built a strong leadership team at the Denver headquarters of FCFI. The secretary was Terry Nieman, a firefighter from Colorado. John R. Barker continued to serve as treasurer. Bill Guindon traveled extensively as FCFI's liaison with firefighters across the United States and Canada.

## Outreach to Firefighters

Under Bob's inspiration and urging FCFI became a strong outreach organization. For instance, the Dallas, TX chapter ministered regularly at the famous burn center of Parkland Hospital. One recalls that President Kennedy died at the trauma center of Parkland Hospital in 1963, after Lee Harvey Oswald shot him. The very active Dallas chapter also gave away $500 worth of toys to needy children at Christmas time.

Bob kept urging the members to be evangelists. "Sometime you will encounter Christians at a fire, training exercise, or other fire department activities. Don't let those opportunities pass. Check to see what the Lord is doing in their lives." The discipleship training Bob received from the Navigators indelibly marked his life and ministry. [19] He challenged every member of FCFI to be an ambassador for Christ.

In order to spread the ministry, the Pike's Peak chapter of FCFI launched a Christian tape ministry. Bob urged chapters to order these Christian cassette tapes and distribute them. Within a few years the Pike's Peak chapter distributed no less than 500 tapes.

In 1990 Bob announced that several chapters had taken responsibility for various outreach ministries. Pike's Peak would continue to head the tape distribution. The Edmonton, Alberta chapter in Canada made ministry cards available, and chapters sent these to firefighters in time of need or celebration. The Sacramento chapter handled the card ministry in the United States. Cards were designed for special events which are: promotion, retirement, birth of a baby, get well, and sympathy in time of grief. The Washington, D.C. chapter adopted the tract outreach. Dee Yates from Greenville, SC coordinated the Prayer Chain. An FCFI Wives Auxiliary sprang up thanks to the Hampton, VA chapter.

From Dallas, TX Ronnie Dobbs described their special fund to help uniformed and non-uniformed personnel. As an example, they enabled a department secretary to attend her mother's funeral. According to Ronnie, this fund experienced "phenomenal growth," as Christian firefighters gave generously to meet the needs of their colleagues.

An especially powerful outreach of FCFI is providing financial assistance for members in need. One firefighter wrote in early 1990: "My wife and I would like to take this opportunity to thank you and hope you can extend our gratitude to the donor who sent money to us." Then the correspondent added, "We have recently been in financial difficulties…[But] God has blessed us beyond what we ever expected." [20] This quiet, gracious sharing has been an earmark of FCFI from the first.

In the same generous way, a work team of 38 firefighters and 4 EMTs set off for Morgan City, LA. There they repaired homes for the elderly, the sick, and the poor. In the process of this mission trip, the team re-roofed six homes, built an extra room on another house, as well as a shed for yet another family. The response throughout Morgan City was so encouraging, as the folks said: "The Lord must have sent y'all down here!" [21]

One of the most touching reports during Bob Crum's presidency came from Arizona. A prisoner at the Arizona State Prison wrote saying: "I am currently incarcerated...and am a member of the fire department here. I would like to receive a copy of *The Encourager*, if that is possible." So, the ministry of FCFI reached even inside prison walls.

To extend his outreach, Bob enlisted Bill Guindon as a traveling representative for FCFI. Even as the chapters were thriving across the country and around the world, Bill began in 1989 traveling on behalf of the FCFI. He was given the title, Fire Service Liaison. Because of his leadership training background, Bill concentrated on building strong leadership conferences for the FCFI on a regular basis. Originally he came from the Astoria, OR Fire Department where he was part of a Leadership Development program led by the Navigators at Glen Eyrie.

Bob Crum surveyed the chapters booking dates for Bill Guindon's visits. Bill Guindon also made frequent visits to chapters in Canada. During his first year he covered more than 8,000 miles and visited forty different chapters. This incessant travel paid off in rapid growth of new chapters. At the same time Duncan and Mary Jane Wilkie were still visiting chapters across the United States.

<u>Family Camps Multiply</u>

By 1985 this ministry began to multiply. From the beginning FCFI leaders had conducted a family camp in Colorado. Sometimes it was set in Estes Park at the YMCA campground, other times it met in Golden, Colorado.

The format was always the same: daily doses of strong Bible teaching and plenty of fellowship time for the firefighter families. Plenty of fun came from an active sports program. Each evening there was a campfire, where families could share with each other.

The purpose of this family camp was simple: to strengthen families in the fire service. In 1985 the divorce rate had reached one marriage in every two. In the fire service the incidence of divorce was even higher. Consequently Bob Crum and his central leadership team focused heavily on the Colorado family camp. The unofficial chaplain of FCFI, Pastor Byron MacDonald, often spoke at the Colorado family camp.

In that same year a second family camp emerged in the Smokey Mountains at Black Mountain, North Carolina. Burt DeLong was the main Bible teacher, and a brother-sister team of Bob and Sissy Miles led the youth ministry. In each case the focus was placed unashamedly on developing the Christian family. Bob and Doris Crum travelled cross-country to be part of the Black Mountain Family Camp.

The relaxed atmosphere of family camps enabled marriage partners to focus on each other, far away from the sound of scanners and pagers, far out of the reach of the local fire department. One firefighter from South Carolina summarized the impact of family camp, when he wrote to Bob Crum: "Please don't make our family wait another year to be blessed by you and your presence at the Eastern Family Camp." [22]

After the Black Mountain Camp, a South Carolina firefighter wrote to FCFI headquarters and thanked them for the camp. Then he added: "This is what heaven is going to be like." For many members of FCFI the family camps had become a lifeline not only for their marriage, but also for their personal walk with the Lord.

Incidentally, Black Mountain is very near to Montreat, North Carolina, where Billy and Ruth Graham made their home. In the village of Black Mountain Billy Graham founded a Christian radio station that has persisted in airing the best in Bible teaching and Christian music for several decades.

<u>A Chapter in Every State and Country</u>

During the presidency of Bob Crum local chapters of FCFI thrived. One year Bob and Doris Crum traveled to visit the Blue Ridge chapter in Greenville, S C immediately after the Black Mountain Family Camp. This chapter took seriously its responsibility to reach the area for the Lord.

Each year the Blue Ridge chapter sponsored a booth at the South Carolina State Firefighter Convention. It was often held at Myrtle Beach, a vacation mecca on the South Carolina shore. From the booth they were able to make connections to start additional chapters and also to place Bibles in firehouses throughout the state.

"You are a vital part of our mission force," Bob Crum reminded the chapters constantly. He was single-minded in his commitment to see active chapters in every state throughout the United States and in every country in the world. Bob never gave an inch on this commitment. He truly believed that the fire departments of the world could be reached for the Lord Jesus Christ, and he powerfully urged the American chapters to take the lead.

In order to spread the word, Bob turned to Ray Richards, general manager of Christian radio station KCMI-FM-104 in Nebraska. Ray put together testimonies from converted firefighters and packaged them to be aired as public service announcements on Christian stations across the country.

Consequently the chapters compounded and grew during Bob Crum's presidency. For instance, in Sacramento, CA Christian firefighters invited their colleagues to meet for breakfast and discuss the founding of a FCFI chapter. At the first breakfast event eighteen firefighters showed up. The Sacramento chapter was born.

From Lethbridge, Alberta, Ed Krajewski wrote to headquarters. The Lethbridge chapter held a weekly breakfast Bible study followed by a time of prayer for the fire service in that Canadian city. Ed needed more FCFI Bibles for distribution to the members of the Lethbridge Fire Department.

A Texas chapter asked for special prayer. Apparently it was a rather small department, but the FCFI leader for that community asked that fellow-members of the fellowship join him in praying for twenty new members in that chapter during 1990.

From Meriden, CT came a letter. In 1991 Firefighter David Bowen attended FDIC in Cincinnati, where he had picked up materials necessary to start a FCFI chapter. When he returned he enlisted fellow-firefighters as well as the department chaplain, Wayne Detzler, to launch a new chapter. Bowen added in his letter: "Chapter meetings reinforce the truth that we are not alone in our mission for Christ." As we write this book, David Bowen is now Deputy Chief of the Meriden Fire Department, where he continues to live out the Christian life.

From Charlotte, NC Keith Helms corresponded with FCFI headquarters. He launched a chapter in the Charlotte Fire Department. As the chapter grew, so did Keith Helms. He progressed from Captain to Battalion Chief, and he spurred on the local chapter throughout his career. When he retired he devoted almost full-time to the local chapter and international ministry of FCFI.

Across the world news of FCFI also spread. One Australian firefighter visited New Zealand, where someone gave him an FCFI video. Later that firefighter returned to his home department in Canberra, Australia. There he set about starting a chapter of FCFI.

The rapid reproduction of FCFI chapters confirmed both the mission and the passion of Bob and Doris Crum. Bob was committed to seeing several chapters in every state here in the United States. By the same token he was intent on multiplying the ministry across the world, so that every country might ha0ve a chapter of FCFI.

The Navigators heavily influenced Bob Crum. The founder of the Navigators was Dawson Trotman, who taught the principles of spiritual multiplication in his little booklet, *Born to Reproduce* (Colorado Springs: NavPress, 1998). Bob Crum caught the vision and applied it vigorously to the fire service as he led FCFI.

## A Bible in Every Firehouse

From earliest days FCFI was committed to place Bibles in firehouses. Reports of this ministry flooded the pages of *The Encourager*. The stories that spring from Bible distribution are thrilling. Already by the year 1985, more than 6,000 Bibles had been placed in firehouses. And God's Word worked.

Kevin Coffey wrote in 1985 on behalf of the Chicago Fire Department FCFI chapter: "I want to express my deepest gratitude to you for your part in getting us started three years ago with the gift of 100 Bibles for our firehouses." [23]

From Groton, CT, home of the U.S. Navy Submarine Base, Chaplain Art Greenleaf wrote stating he had presented a Bible to Chief Robert Burdick, when the new Poquonnock Volunteer Fire Department opened its first station. Chief Burdick responded: "The first book I want in my station is the Bible."

The Bibles even crossed over to other services. Dick Arndt wrote from the Behavioral Science Unit at the FBI Academy in Quantico, VA. When Arndt moved into his new office, he found a box full of FCFI Bibles. They had sat there for some time. Arndt commented, "I opened it [the box] and was tickled silly to see all those Bibles."

From the California Department of Forestry and Fire Prevention came a note of thanks for Bibles distributed to their training facility. The correspondent added that each year 2,000 new firefighters are trained, and they want to place a Bible in every dormitory room.

From Irving, TX came some advanced plans which included the Bibles. The Irving Department was recruiting new members, and a correspondent asked for Bibles to be placed in new firehouses that would be opened.

Even small volunteer departments profited from the placement of Bibles. An illustration came from the Citizens Volunteer Fire Company of Fawn Grove, PA. They had received two Bibles: one for the main firehouse and one for the substation.

By 1988 word came from Spokane, WA asking for replacement Bibles. The original copies given to that department were "all worn out." So, we can see that the Bibles were read by firefighters, at least in Spokane.

One of the most thrilling reports comes from the Washington, D.C. Fire Department. A firefighter recounted that he was not sure God existed or that God loved him, but his situation was hopeless. So, he opened the firehouse Bible and prayed: "God, if you really exist, I give you my life. Take it and do with it what you will." This firefighter became a bright witness for Christ throughout his life. [24]

Only eternity will tell how great the impact of Bible distribution in firehouses has been across America and around the world. Certainly many seeking firefighters have found the Lord through reading God's Word.

The Lord provided for the needs of FCFI as they sent the Word of God into firehouses. By 1987, giving to FCFI totaled $36,486.06. Two years later giving grew to $44,794.36. To the eternal credit of Bob Crum and his leadership team, they used every cent to spread the gospel throughout the fire service.

## Bob Crum's Presidency Finishes

Early in 1992 John Barker left the leadership team to take on a missionary assignment. He became a member of the crew of the Mercy Ships that extends Christian care around the world. John's ability to manage funds enabled him to organize the finances of the ship ministry.

At the end of 1992, Bob Crum wrote a very moving letter of resignation to the Board of FCFI. In part he said: "The Fellowship is now at a point of needing to move forward and I am not capable of providing the leadership to accomplish the task….I am thankful for the support, encouragement, and love you have given me in my ministry. I love you all." Bob's dear wife, Doris, died in November 1992 after a prolonged illness.

Duncan Wilkie stepped in to take up the slack. He built a leadership team with Walt Gabbert as vice president, Terry Neiman as secretary/treasurer, and Bill Guindon as the FCFI Liaison.

Duncan spoke for the entire fellowship, when he wrote in the November-December 1992 issue of *The Encourager*: "My brother Bob Crum has suffered much over the past year due to the long illness of his beloved wife Doris. Her passing has been very hard. Bob has written a letter to all members in the Nov/Dec Encourager… Bob Crum has been a man of prayer. And I know his heart is with you all… I thank my God for Bob. He has been so very faithful to our Lord in encouraging all of us in our daily walk. Thank you Bob." [25]

# Chapter 4

## Bill Guindon (1993-94)—Triumph through Transition

Although Bob Crum did not resign formally until December 1992, Bill Guindon had long been a familiar face to FCFI chapters and their leaders. After serving with the Astoria, OR fire department Bill relocated to Colorado Springs, where he entered a Navigator leadership program.

While reading *Firehouse* magazine Bill became acquainted with the ministry of the Fellowship of Christian Firefighters. Because of his background in the fire service Bill also soon discovered the Pikes Peak chapter of FCFI, and he became part of that chapter. He often led Bible studies for the firefighters and this wet his taste for the ministry in FCFI.

In 1989 Bill was appointed to the position of Fire Service Liaison and given the responsibility of connecting with chapters across the country and in Canada. Bill's strong skill was developing relationships with firefighters and their families. This strengthened the connection of fellowship between the widely scattered members. In this role he quickly became the face of the Fellowship of Christian Firefighters for many members.

## At Home and Away

Although Bill's base was at the FCFI headquarters in Denver, more often than not he was traveling between chapters. He quickly won the hearts of the members, because he listened to them and counseled them. Most of all he prayed with and for them.

When Bill married Pam in 1991 they became a team in every way. Pam assisted in the office, while Bill visited firefighters. He traveled thousands of miles each year touching base with members of the Fellowship. In every case he sought to deepen their commitment to the Lord and broaden their impact on the fire service. The modest amount needed for monthly support came in, and Bill and Pam were able to devote all their energy to ministry within the fire service.

Not only did Bill Guindon cultivate relationships with the members of FCFI, he also urged them to connect with local pastors. In a special article published in *The Encourager* Bill wrote: "One of the greatest resources available in many communities is your pastor."

He urged firefighters to invite pastors to a meal at the firehouse, even to take them on a "ride along" in the fire truck. No pastor could resist that! Here Wayne Detzler's personal testimony is applicable. It was a fire captain that applied this approach to Detzler, who was then his pastor in Meriden, Connecticut. The captain's contact led to more than twenty years of service as a fire chaplain.

Furthermore, Bill suggested that the members invite their pastors to training events, where they could experience the skills of firefighting firsthand. One pastor in Trumbull, CT took this so seriously that he became a firefighter, as well as a chaplain. Bill urged members to give their pastor regular issues of the *Encourager* as a constant connecting point.

Because Bill had first learned about FCFI through the advertisement in *Firehouse Magazine*, he persisted in placing similar notices. In 1993 he inserted a series of advertisements that brought a significant increase in FCFI membership. Across the world firefighters read the advertisements, and correspondence in the files attests to the popularity of this program.

Later that year Bill wrote a major article for the *Encourager*. In this piece he expounded on the primary purpose of FCFI, to encourage Christian firefighters in their faith. He reminded the membership of the key verses: "And let us consider one another to provoke unto love and to good works: Not forsaking the assembling of ourselves together, as the manner of some is; but exhorting one another: and so much the more, as ye see the day approaching." (Heb. 10:24-25)

Bill drew out three main challenges within this key passage. First, our job is to encourage believers in the fire service, wherever we may find them. Second, our task is equipping Christian firefighters for their witness in the fire service. Third, we challenge firefighters to stand up and be counted for the Lord within the fire service. He concluded by writing: "I challenge you to consider how you may stimulate others in impacting the fire service for Christ." [26]

Early in 1994 it became clear that FCFI offices would be forced to move. The owner of their building decided to sell the premises, and this necessitated a move from the original office in Denver. Although the headquarters would remain in Denver, they would need a new facility. Bill and Pam Guindon faced the challenge of finding new space.

By 1994 Bill and Pam were alone in serving the headquarters of the Fellowship. Duncan Wilkie became interim president when Bob Crum resigned at the end of 1992. Soon thereafter Duncan was called to the position of interim pastor. Likewise, others moved on to new ministries, and so Bill and Pam were on their own. *The Encourager* included no names other than Bill as FCFI Liaison with the fire service.

When asked recently to describe the strength of FCFI, Bill remained single minded. He wrote: "I believe prayer and relationships which promote encouragement to firefighters and their families are a wonderful strength of FCFI." Then he added, *"The Encourager provides inspiration and encouragement and in many cases a testimony of being a Christian firefighter."* [27]

When asked to assess the strength of FCFI, Bill wrote the following perceptive paragraph: "FCF plays in the spiritual development of firefighters and their families. When FCF becomes the local church or provides the same services as a local church the impact on the fire service mission field can be minimized. I believe it is very important to ensure that the mission of FCF is clear and consistent. FCF has a specific target audience few can ever reach but Christian firefighters and their families." [28]

The heartbeat of FCFI must always be encouraging firefighters to live for Christ while in the fire service. This spilled out to their families and to their communities and becomes a bright and shining light for the Lord in the tough world of firefighting.

### Chapters Multiply and Flourish

The pages of *The Encourager* remind the reader of the rapid growth in FCFI during the early 1990s. Much of this expansion was due to ceaseless encouragement by Bill and Pam Guindon. Its amazing depth only matches the diversity of this growth.

<u>U.S. Navy.</u> From the decks of the USS John F. Kennedy came a letter. The author was a "Damage Controlman," a firefighter on board the aircraft carrier. Since joining the Navy he had "put his faith on the back burner." Then he picked up a copy of *Firehouse* magazine and came across the FCFI ad. This apparently coincidental contact with FCFI led him back to the Lord. He wrote to solidify his connection with the Fellowship. [29]

<u>California Forestry Service.</u> Another strong contact came from the California Forestry Service and their firefighting division. Steve Seltzner wrote: "Five years ago it seemed like there were no Christians in the Forest Service at all. And now it seems God is rising up an army…. As we prepare for the 1994 'Fire Season' and hire on new troops, we look forward to more opportunities to share Jesus."

Then he pled: "Send me a bunch of pocket New Testaments." Seltzner signed his letter, "fireproof in Him." [30]

Fire Chief Dean R. Lucke wrote from the Department of Forestry and Fire Protection in San Mateo, CA. He requested twenty-five FCFI Bibles, one for each of the stations and facilities in his ranger unit.

<u>Sacramento</u>. Jeff and Karen Lynch wrote on behalf of the Sacramento Fire Department. They were discouraged by meager attendance at prayer breakfasts during 1992, but early in 1993 things picked up. They reported that twenty-two attended the prayer breakfasts and they shared how God had worked during the tough year of 1992. Jeff and Karen were encouraged about the prospect of serving God in the new year of 1993.

<u>Sharon, PA</u>. Many other references to the *Firehouse* magazine ads dot the pages of FCFI publications. Tony Zarella wrote from Sharon, PA. For many years he had been the only identified believer in the local fire department, than Terry Whalen was hired. Terry saw an ad in *Firehouse* magazine and linked up with Tony. They quickly became known as the "Bible Buddies" of the firehouse. [31]

Another Pennsylvania firefighter contacted FCFI. Two years previously he had picked up the firehouse Bible, a gift from FCFI. As he read it he turned to the Lord in faith. In 1994 he wrote asking how to launch a chapter of FCFI in his town. [32]

<u>Frankfort, KY</u>. Kentucky also became a fertile field for FCFI as chapters began to spring up. G. R. Pennington was fire chief in

Frankfort, KY. The chief himself took the lead in contacting FCFI and seeking information on establishing a chapter in his department. It is ironic that many times it was the chiefs, who took the initiative of introducing FCFI to their departments during the early years.

Hawesville, KY. Writing from a volunteer department in rural Hawesville, KY, Rick Cox told of learning about FCFI. He was teaching at the Institute of Emergency Management at Emmitsburg, MD. One evening he picked up the Bible placed by FCFI at the academy. He wrote to headquarters seeking information on starting a chapter of FCFI in his department.

Washington, D.C. Over the years one of the most consistent chapters has been in Washington, D.C. As early as 1992 a correspondent wrote: "I am excited about our regular monthly breakfast; attendance was wonderful! We had twenty-two people including our new chief. Praise God." [33]

South Carolina. From the Bible Belt in South Carolina interest in FCFI also flourished during the 1990s. A volunteer firefighter told of receiving Bibles and starting an FCFI chapter in his county. He added: "There are about one hundred fifty believing firefighters in this county. The harvest is ripe!" [34]

Another South Carolina firefighter explained he had led several firefighters to the Lord and discipled them. Now he was eager to launch a chapter of FCFI for his particular county.

Clemson, SC. From the Tri-County chapter near Clemson, SC came a report that tract racks and Bibles had been placed in each of the firehouses. It seemed as if there was no limit to the work that could be accomplished by FCFI in South Carolina.

<u>Palm Beach, FL.</u> Florida represented a similar story. David Lewis wrote on behalf of the Palm Beach City Fire Rescue service. He had received a video presenting the work of FCFI. This became part of the recruit-training curriculum for Palm Beach. Additionally, the fire department included the FCFI video in its training program on local public access television. Lewis concluded: "The video has been piped into every firehouse and home in the area. [35]

<u>Sarasota, FL.</u> From Sarasota, FL firefighter Randy Patterson reported to FCFI headquarters. He had discovered a Bible at the Ocala State Fire College. When he returned home he launched chapters in several Florida fire departments. [36]

<u>Orlando, FL.</u> Another powerful connector for FCFI members was the fellowship-wide prayer chain. Sam Thurmond from Orlando, FL called to report on a police officer, who had been struck down by a car and injured badly. Patterson wrote: "I want to express my deepest thanks and gratitude for the quick activation of the Prayer Chain." The officer was recovering from his severe injuries, and Sam Thurmond wanted to give God the glory for this. [37]

<u>Radford, VA.</u> Another unusual contact for the Fellowship came from the Radford (VA) Army Ammunition Plant. David Pannell, Jr. was crew chief for the in house fire department at the plant. He requested and received FCFI Bibles for his station. He wrote to say: "What a blessing your Bibles were to our department." [38]

Dallas, TX. The spiritual impact of FCFI is enormous. Brief glimpses arise from the vigorous correspondence in the files of headquarters. From Dallas, TX a Senior Fire and Rescue Officer, Steve Bohannan, tells the story: "I am returning to walk with our Lord and Savior. For several years I have turned my back on my Heavenly Father and thanks to much prayer from my family and organizations such as ours [FCFI] I have turned around and now am walking toward and with Jesus." [39] This letter is a prime example of one of the strongest ministries FCFI has had over the years, to be an encouragement for Christians in their walk with the Lord while in the fire service.

Meriden, CT. The Meriden, CT chapter was launched by a couple of firefighters and their chaplain, Wayne Detzler. The spark plug of that chapter was Firefighter Mark Stefanski. In late 1992 he encouraged FCFI headquarters with this note: "Keep up the good work. I appreciate your ministry to firefighters. I can see God working in 'cold' New England. God is moving by His Spirit, but one thing I know, He wants me to spend more time in prayer." [40]

Allendale, MI. Like Stefanski, some firefighters had a regional vision for the ministry of FCFI. One such big vision person was Jim Harker from Allendale, MI. He had established a small chapter in his department, but now he focused on reaching all of Western Michigan. He asked for the privilege of becoming the FCFI's contact person for the entire Grand Rapids area. [41]

## Bill Guindon's Ministry in Perspective

Although Bill and Pam had invested several years their lives and energy in the work of FCFI, it was their relationships that best illustrated their impact. Almost every FCFI chapter profited from Bill's personal attention. In fact, his personal goal was just that: to touch every chapter and encourage the members.

On behalf of the FCFI Board, Ken Vaughan summarized Bill and Pam's ministry in this catchy paragraph: "Lousy pay and long hours—what more could you ask?" Why do Bill and Pam persist? "Because they love the Lord and have a desire to share the love of Christ through ministry in the fire service." [42] Ken Vaughn was an engineer with the Aurora, CO Fire Department, and he experienced Bill and Pam's ministry firsthand.

When asked to put his ministry into perspective, Bill Guindon responded: "I believe I was an instrument used by God to develop relationships particularly with chapter leaders. Much of my time was spent counseling, listening, and most important praying." [43] At the end of Bill's time of ministry he wrote a letter stating that he believed the ministry had come to an end. Within this letter Bill resigned from leading FCFI as the Fire Liaison.

## A Time of Transition

Even though the leaders at this time believed FCFI was finished God had other plans. Two Fort Collins Poudre Fire chapter members, Randy Mirowski and Ron Lindroth, along with Pastor Steve Ratzlaff from Livermore Volunteer Fire Department, stepped into the leadership role to continue the ministry. These three dedicated members understood that FCFI was God's ministry and met to pray for God's guidance. They contacted Gay Reynolds, also from the Livermore Volunteer Fire Department, and set a meeting at the Denver office with retiring board members Walt Gabbert, acting treasurer Terry Nieman and several others. As a result of that meeting, and most of all God's direction, a new era for the fellowship was launched. Randy Mirowski agreed to serve on the board as president to handle the board responsibilities.

# Chapter 5

## Gaius Reynolds (1995-2012)—Restoring the Reach

It was in 1995 that Gay Reynolds and his wife, Sue, accepted the position of missionaries for the Fellowship of Christian Firefighters International. Sue served as editor of the newsletter, and Gay served as the missionary and later missionary/president of FCFI until January, 2013.

The story of their involvement in FCFI dates back to early 1994. Gay and Sue were living in California where he owned and operated a retail business while Sue, after teaching at the elementary through college level, was serving as director of children's ministries at a large non-denominational church. Both of their children were planning to marry that year and live in Colorado. Their shared dream was to someday live in the mountains, and Colorado sounded like the place for them to move now. The fact that their children were in Colorado was an added incentive. The Reynolds sold the business, Sue resigned, and they prayed for God to lead them to a place in the mountains, to a Bible teaching church, and to open the doors for them to go into ministry together.

They serve a God who does answer prayer. After the Reynolds built their home in the mountains they found a local Bible based church. Gay joined the Livermore Volunteer Fire Department where he acquired an EMT certification and later accepted the position of chief.

The current board members consisted of Terry Neiman, Ken Vaughn, Charles Barela, Walt Gabbert, Randy Mirowski, and Ron Lindroth. Terry Neiman, Ken Vaughn, Charles Barela, and Walt Gabbert stepped down from leadership at the same time as Bill Guindon. Most of these members continued to support FCFI through the years, ensuring that this ministry continued to be God's ministry to firefighters.

Gay and Sue knew that a challenge was ahead of them. Nevertheless, they agreed to commit to serving as volunteers for one year to see if the FCFI ministry was God's will. God's will soon revealed itself to the membership. FCFI member, Harry Hetz, donated the funding for a much needed computer. Members called and encouraged Gay and Sue that FCFI was God's ministry, and Pastor Steve, Randy Mirowski, and Ron Lindroth worked alongside them to help gain a greater understanding of FCFI. The new leadership developed a vision and mission focus teams from around the country. Mark Sprenger, a retired Poudre Authority Firefighter and FCFI member, joined the board in 1996 and served until 2002. Pastor Steve remained on the board until 2002 when he moved to a new church to minister. Gay and Sue's one-year commitment turned into seventeen faithful years.

The Reynolds said this while reflecting on the past, "it is with thankfulness to God to see how He continues to grow this, His ministry, and to bless many in the fire service including firefighters, emergency medical personnel, and dispatchers through the Fellowship."

## Equipping the Called

It has been said that God doesn't call the equipped; He equips those He calls. In regards to Gay and Sue this was true. When the search committee was formed in 2010 to replace the Reynolds, they realized that if they were required to go through such a committee, they might never have been selected. In the beginning Gay and Sue didn't even know what FCFI was and here they were heading up the ministry. Gay had firefighters working for him while he had only been a volunteer for a few months, but God's ways aren't our ways, and Gay and Sue both had willing hearts to serve Him wherever He placed them.

After the Reynolds moved the office to their home they studied what items were inherited. Within a short time Sue was asked when the newsletter would come out. They both looked at each other: What newsletter? Again God equipped them and the first newsletter was published several weeks later. It began as the traditional six page newsletter and as more members caught the vision and shared God's faithfulness in their lives, it grew to eight pages in September of 1998, to twelve pages by November of 2001, and then again to sixteen pages later in July of 2002. As more members and chapters contributed articles and updates, it was obvious that the newsletter needed to adapt to their interests and willingness to encourage one another. In November 2011, the first color edition was printed. At the recommendation of the board, the *Encourager* was made available by e-mail and nearly four hundred people receive their issue by e-mail. Over eighteen hundred continue to receive it by mail.

As Gay and Sue continued to search the files in those early years, they came across the original purpose and statement of beliefs (which is stated in chapter 1) established by FCFI's founders which reflected their beliefs. These were as follows:

**The FCFI Purpose**: Glorifying God in the fire service, fellowshipping together for individual growth in the Christian life, serving the cause of Christ through the church of one's own choice, encouraging those in the fire service in their Christian life, sharing locally in planned fellowship meetings, individual contact, and prayer, bringing all Christians in the fire service to a common goal of praying for the fire service and its members, sharing on an international basis through an annual international conference, having contact internationally with fellow Christian firefighters, and the caring for firefighters in times of need.

Individual chapters and members share Christ's love in the fire service and their communities in many other and varied ways.

## Family Camp

Gay and Sue learned that FCFI had a Family Camp. Their role in helping organize it and attending were part of the international's expectations. Pastor Steve agreed to be the speaker and off they went to Asheville, NC. During their first trip to family camp they met many long-standing members and were blessed to know that they would willingly coordinate future Family Camps. Those members have faithfully continued to minister to first responders at Family Camp since their first one.

## Meeting With The Founders And Existing Board

While initially going through the office items, Gay discovered one of the founders, Bob Crum, resided in Denver. They met with him and then set up a later date to meet both Duncan Wilkie and John Barker, also part of the founding leadership. Much information and great insights were gleaned from these meetings.

In the early years of Gay and Sue's leadership, Ron Lindroth hosted a meeting at his mountain cabin and invited all current board members, presidents, and interested members to attend. The turnout was not large, but several came from the local area, as well as, one from Missouri and one from Indiana providing Gay and Sue with more valuable insights and direction.

Gay and Sue followed up the meetings with the still existing board members Ron Lindroth, Randy Mirowski, and the newly recruited board members Mark Sprenger and Pastor Steve Ratliff. Out came the dry erase board and a brainstorming session followed. All who attended shared the desire to see FCFI continue to reach out to the fire service with God's love, peace, and truth. The uniqueness of this profession in it's shift scheduling, as well as, the physical and emotional demands faced by first responders dealing with tragedy and loss on a daily basis have caused far too many to turn to addictive habits. Being aware that only through Christ and His death on the cross can one have eternal life, it was unanimously voted on to establish the FCFI vision as Philippians 3:10a: "That I may know him and the power of His resurrection." (KJV) It was also decided to taking this vision to the fire service community by *Evangelism*, *Empowerment*, and *Encouragement.* This became the FCFI mission statement; a mission that hundreds of FCFI members continue to actively pursue.

The next goal was to develop a solid base of leadership, to train up and recruit additional leaders who believe in FCFI's vision and mission. Gay and Sue knew that the broader the leadership base, the more successful FCFI would become. Having leaders who are involved and share the vision and mission would also ensure that when the next leadership transition occurred, qualified leadership would be in place.

The existing board supported Gay and Sue as they developed a plan to recruit an International Board from members in different parts of the country, members who would encourage local members and leaders in their areas via personal contact, e-mail, or phone conferences. Along with establishing an International Board expansion, a plan was set in place to recruit regional directors to represent their local areas. These new Regional Directors would encourage chapter presidents and firefighters on a more personal and area appropriate level (Hebrews 10:25). Regional Directors could also represent FCFI in local churches, fire departments, conferences, and expositions. Inherent in developing a team of leaders, was the need to establish a broad avenue for new input for the efficient administration and outreach of all of FCFI. By 2001 God had called twelve dedicated firefighters to serve as regional directors. His timing is always perfect and when the Attack on America took the lives of 343 firefighters, FCFI had a strong leadership network in place to help.

There was nothing good about The Attack on America; it was a vicious enemy attack on the land we love. It took the lives of many citizens as well as those willing to lay down their lives for others (John 15:13). But God promises that good can come from the worst of situations, and FCFI has always been a recipient of God's goodness.

## God Uses All Things For His Glory

Romans 8:28 states: "And we know that all things work together for the good to them that love God, to them who are called according to his purpose."

A change in the International Board occurred during this time when Pastor Steve moved to plant a new church and Mark Sprenger and Randy Mirowski resigned from the board later that year. Dave Chapman came on in the interim and served until 2003 when he and

Ron Lindroth resigned contingent on new leadership stepping forward.

By this time, Gay and Sue had traveled to many conferences and extended their trips to visit as many local members and chapters as they could along the way. They met a strong core of members with a heart for the Lord who had been sharing their testimony with other firefighters in hopes they would know Him. Gay and Sue prayed that God would send a slate of International Board Members from across the country and He did just that. God sent in 2002 Raul Angulo from Washington State, Pastor Ken Hall from Colorado, Tommy Neiman from Florida, and Dan Clegg from Indiana. Then in 2003 God sent Lee Callahan from Massachusetts. Through the years expanding and replacing the board has been an ongoing process with Russ Stammer from New Jersey and Craig Duck from Maryland coming on board.

George Rabiela, who previously served as a regional director, retired from the Chicago Fire Department and expanded his outreach to Mexico. In 2009 he was appointed as the Mexico Outreach Director. Rick Barton, a faithful contributor to *The Encourager*, traveled the country extensively as a wildland safety officer and speaker. He shared FCFI and gave away hundreds of *Bibles* and *Stories of Faith and Courage* devotionals. In 2009 he became FCFI's Ambassador-At-Large. In 2011, Frank Schaper, who conducts training sessions nationwide, became FCFI's Outreach Director.

Gay and Sue's prayers continued for more FCFI members to catch the vision and join the leadership team. A major goal was to help members understand that they are FCFI and are an important vessel of God's to bring His love, Word, peace, and truth to the fire service.

Equally important has been the underlying truth that the fire service is a unique profession. Gay and Sue believed the fire service to include medics, dispatchers, and fire fighters. FCFI's ministry has been geared to all first responders, and is open to all who share the vision and statement of belief established by the founders and based on God's Holy Word. First responders face tragedy and destruction on an often daily basis. The founders realized, and Gay and Sue have personally witnessed first hand over the years, how without the Lord, many first responders seek other ways to help them deal with the losses encountered in this profession.

Drug, alcohol, and pornography addictions coupled with a high rate of divorce are often the chosen avenue. Post traumatic stress disorder (PTSD) is not uncommon. But there is a way, a narrow way according to Scripture that is available to all. That way is through Jesus Christ. Is it easy to be a Christian in this highly secular and worldly profession? If the testimonies heard frequently hold any bearing, the answer is an unarguable "No". Is it possible? Yes. The question the past and future leadership is faced with is, how can FCFI help those who have accepted Christ continue to walk with God and share His love?

## Growth in the Ministry

During the years that Gay and Sue served the membership as the President/Missionary of FCFI God blessed their work. They were able to take the ministry from almost extinction to a thriving organization. Their passion was to minister to first responders who have accepted Christ as Lord and Savior and to encourage them to continue to walk with Him. Over the next seventeen years Gay and Sue saw God's blessing on the fire service.

Fire conferences that were attended by FCFI grew from two in the early days to six. Local chapters were also attending conferences and fire schools in their area. Prayers of local leaders being developed for use in their area was realized as more and more were stepping up to help. With all of the new conferences came a desire for new resources to be developed. Bible studies as well as several books were made available due to Sue's God given talents as an editor.

After the events of September 11th God continued to open doors for FCFI and Gay and Sue were not afraid to walk through them. A New Testament was developed by IBS, now Biblica, with the help of Sue. These were specifically designed with first responders in mind. With Sue's help members were able to have their stories read by many first responders all over the world. God also opened the door for a devotional book, *Stories of Faith and Courage from Firefighters and First Responders,* to be developed and published with God's divine help. FCFI members from around the country submitted articles to the International Office and Sue compiled them for the 365 devotions. Many first responders have been encouraged in their faith as a result of this devotional book.

As technology began to increase Gay and Sue had faithful members who were willing to improve the ministry. The prayer chain became electronic, a web site was developed, a Facebook page was started, and the vision was spread faster than at any other time in FCFI history. God has always used people to accomplish His purpose and FCFI was no exception. Gay and Sue brought their expertise of networking to FCFI and the ministry began to network with other like-minded ministries in order to spread the gospel in the fire service. It is only known by God how many first responders were "stirred up" during these years of FCFI.

### A Time For Change

It has been said that all good things must come to an end. When Gay and Sue read a letter of resignation at one of the board meetings all were saddened at the thought of Gay and Sue leaving the ministry. Gay described it this way when asked about the ministry: "My wife and I were blessed to serve in this, God's ministry, for seventeen years. We are a prime example of how God can take the least likely servants and use them for His glory. We fully believe that God called us to the FCFI ministry and we are equally certain that it was His will that FCFI move on to a new era. We look forward to seeing what God has planned for the new president, Craig Duck, and his expanding and dedicated FCFI board. We look forward to our role as board members, but most of all we look forward to seeing how

God uses FCFI in the future. Craig has many innovative ideas as well as a willingness to continue the programs developed in response to your—the member's input. Remember you are FCFI, and your input and involvement have been instrumental in taking the vision of knowing Christ too many in the fire service."

# Chapter 6

## What's an "Encourager?"

The story goes that when Gay and Sue Reynolds assumed leadership of FCFI someone contacted them and asked about *The Encourager*. Throughout the transition no one had briefed them about this aspect of the work, so they responded, "What's an Encourager?"

Soon, however, Gay and Sue hit their stride, and their masterful handling of *The Encourager* has transformed it into a must-read Christian periodical. The beginnings of this news letter were relatively simple. Only one year passed after the founding of FCFI before Bob Crum issued the first edition of *The Encourager*. He explained the purpose in these words: "What a joy it is for me to be able to share with you for the first time through *The Encourager*. Many of you have waited patiently for this first edition and prayed for us as we tried to get everything organized and operational." [44]

Duncan Wilkie wrote a column as president, in which he cast the vision of FCFI, Bob Crump acting as secretary explained the organizational structure of the ministry, and in the first edition of *The Encourage* the leadership team was introduced. Soon after John Barker, another member of the Denver Fire Department, came alongside as the financial manager and treasurer of FCFI.

## Chapter Highlight

From the beginning Bob included excerpts of letters from chapters across the country and around the world. Many years later he explained the importance of the chapters with fascinating word pictures. The noted Chaplain of the United States Senate, Richard Halvorson, had taught: "We can come together as marbles or as grapes. If we connect as marbles we ricochet off each other without noticeable effect. If we come together as grapes we are crushed and the juices flow together. When we come together with that attitude, willing to be crushed, our fellowship will produce Christian growth." [45]

Very early in the history of *The Encourager* there appeared precise instructions for starting a chapter of FCFI. It explained how firefighters could come together and obtain a charter from FCFI in Denver. The by-laws were readily available, and they gave in-depth instruction on starting a chapter. The initial registration fee in 1979 was only five dollars.

The earliest reports came from Pennsylvania and Louisiana. In the same edition there was a report from Washington, presumably Washington State. Someone read an article about FCFI in *Fire Chief Magazine*. This led to the first breakfast meeting, and six firefighters attended it. Alongside these initial reports, Bob Crum placed the purpose and the activity statement of FCFI. Each issue emphasized the importance of keeping on track, maintaining focus in the ministry of serving Christ within the fire service.

By 1982 *The Encourager* reported that there were thirty-eight chapters operating across America and in other countries. Already it had become the Fellowship of Christian Firefighters International. At the same time the Sacramento chapter assumed responsibility for the greeting card ministry of FCFI. Special cards were designed for promotion or retirement, the birth of a new baby, get well cards for injured or ill firefighters, and sympathy cards for times of bereavement. These cards were supplied a minimal cost by the Sacramento chapter, and they quickly became a major outreach tool of the various chapters of FCFI.

By 1988 the ministry arms of FCFI had been strengthened and lengthened. Sacramento still supplied the greeting cards for use in the fire service. Washington, D.C. assumed responsibility for distributing a line of tracts that contained the testimony of various Christian firefighters. More than twenty years later, these tracts still send a strong message despite their simple layout.

Dee Yates from Greenville, South Carolina assumed responsibility for the FCFI prayer chain. This ministry grew exponentially over the years to come. From the Colorado Springs area a series of videotapes was produced to make known the ministry of FCFI. The Edmonton, Alberta chapter circulated these videos to the Canadian chapters. Duncan Wilkie, the first president, often traveled to Canada to encourage chapters both in the east and in the western provinces. In Hampton, Virginia Phyllis Garris launched the FCFI Wives ministry. This provided encouragement and fellowship for wives of firefighters.

From the perspective of three decades it is encouraging to observe how rapidly the organization of FCFI took shape. Much of this was due to Bob Crum's role in the headquarters and Duncan Wilkie's visionary leadership as the first president. It also testifies to the absolute commitment of our early leaders. Without their dedication to the cause, FCFI would never have grown and blossomed as it has.

## Teaching to Serve

Jesus explained leadership in a revolutionary way. The Bible tells us: "But Jesus called them unto him, and said, Ye know that the princes of the Gentiles exercise dominion over them, and they that are great exercise authority upon them. But it shall not be so among you: but whosoever will be great among you, let him be your minister; And whosoever will be chief among you, let him be your servant" (Matt. 20:25-27)

Bob Crum enlisted Pastor Byron MacDonald to write a strong devotional for each edition of *The Encourager*. Bob introduced the pastor with this glowing statement: "His desire is to see firefighters encouraged and strengthened in their walk with the Lord and other firefighters reached for Christ." Byron had been a pastor in the Denver area since 1980, and he was one of the original members of the FCFI Board of Advisors. [46]

Pastor MacDonald's articles carried the general title of "Looking into God's Word." He dealt with very practical subjects, including a prolonged series on "Overcoming the Enemy," which was sort of a handbook to spiritual warfare. Each time Byron brought the Scripture to bear on life in the fire service.

Byron MacDonald augmented his ministry to FCFI by speaking at various conferences. Sometimes he taught at the leadership retreat at Glen Eyrie. Other times he spoke at the western Family Conference. Each time his ministry was especially well received by the membership of FCFI.

Pastor MacDonald served in the Denver area during most of the 1980s. Then in 1989 he was called to the pulpit of First Baptist Church in Yucaipa, California. Still he continued to write for *The Encourager*. Bob Crum commended the articles with this statement: "He [Pastor MacDonald] is a pastor who knows and has a heart for the fire service." As such, Pastor MacDonald became an example for numerous pastors yet to come as fire chaplains and servants to those who serve as firefighters around the world.

Not only did Bob Crum engage Pastor MacDonald to teach the firefighters, Bob also included strong teaching in his communication. For instance, in 1988 he listed seven "Practical Tips for the Work Place."

1. Work heartily as for the Lord and not just for man. (Col. 3:23)
2. Build loving relationships with unbelievers you work with in anyway you can without compromising personal holiness. (1 Cor. 9:19-23)

3. Separate yourself from anyone, any activity, and any conversation that compromises your striving after personal holiness of mind and body. Recognize and accept the fact that as a Christian you can no longer fit in as "one of the boys" anymore. (2 Cor. 6:14-18)
4. Exercise self-restraint and self-discipline in every area of firehouse living (eating, sleeping, exercising, personal cleanliness, etc.). (1 Cor. 9:27)
5. Confess openly to those you may have offended or compromised with sin in front of them. (Matt. 5:23-24)
6. Open your mouth to speak your testimony and share the Gospel. (rom. 1:16; Acts 1:8)
7. Obey the orders and directives that come from the administration or your employer (this one is not too popular these days!). (Col. 3:22) [47]

"Meet A Member"

Early in the pages of *The Encourager* there appeared a very popular feature, the front-page witness of "Meet a Member." Amazingly each edition carried an in-depth testimony of some member of FCFI. The procurement of these feature stories required nothing less than editorial genius.

Written to a very specific outline, these front-page pieces gave honest and in-depth introductions to members of FCFI. Some were department chiefs, others were working firefighters, and still others were EMTs and administrative personnel. The sole connecting link was participation in the fire service on some level.

Usually the testimony demonstrated a dramatic change in the subject's life. For instance, Chief Kenneth Henry of Brandon, FL was the first subject. He described his spiritual journey from being a hard-drinking sailor to his conversion and his life of faith toward the Lord and faithfulness to his family. [48]

Kevin Coffey told a similar story. His use of alcohol and drugs led to his suspension from the Chicago Fire Department. After Christ got ahold of Kevin this all changed. In 1988 he wrote about his role as an FCFI leader in the large Chicago chapter. [49]

John Barker served as treasurer of FCFI from the very first. In 1991 he retired from the Denver Fire Department with the rank of captain. At the same time he finished his role as treasurer of FCFI, he embarked on a new ministry with the Youth On A Mission aboard Mercy Ships. These ships delivered medical care, dental treatment, construction help, and teachings to countries around the world. For many years John served as the finance officer with great dedication and distinction. He laid out this vision in a "Meet a Member" article in 1991. [50]

Terry Neiman took up the role as secretary/treasurer. He described John Barker's ministry in this moving paragraph: "Since the inception of FCF, he [John] has handled all the finances and has been a trustworthy steward of the money the Lord has provided. He has been a man of strong faith, knowing God would provide for our needs as long as we were following His will." [51]

These columns create a powerful impact on the readers. Because men and women of every level in the fire service write them, they appeal to everyone from the firefighter to the officer and the chief. They also demonstrate how God takes imperfect people to accomplish his perfect work.

## Conferences to Lead and to Live

Early in the ministry of FCFI Bob Crum began organizing conferences. He realized that major steps in discipleship could be taken, if firefighters and their families gathered in an informal, welcoming atmosphere. As early as 1980 a Family Camp was held in Colorado. The nearby peak district proved to be an attractive spot for this original retreat ministry.

Snow Mountain Ranch in Colorado proved to be the best center for family camps, and Bob Crum applied his skills in discipleship to recruit the best Bible teachers available. Pastor Byron MacDonald was one of the first camp speakers, and his popularity with the members of FCFI led to a long relationship with the organization, including his series of Bible studies published in *The Encourager*.

Several years later an east coast family camp was also added. The ideal spot was Christmont, a family-friendly conference center located in Black Mountain, North Carolina. Bob and Doris Crum made the trek cross-country to help lead the first Eastern Family Camp, and that ministry has persisted until the present.

A third conference ministry was the Leadership Training Conference, housed at the Navigator headquarters in Glen Eyrie, Colorado Springs. The availability of Navigator personnel enhanced this ministry, and it persisted for many years as an ideal discipleship opportunity within FCFI.

*The Encourager* proved to be a good medium for promoting these conferences. Not only did the headquarters staff announce the upcoming conferences, but they also carried detailed reports with pictures after each conference. The pages of *the Encourager* often contained a profile of the speakers for each conference, and this enables us to track the history of these powerful spiritual gatherings.

<u>Bill Guindon—FCFI Liaison</u>

In the pages of *The Encourager* a new name appeared. It was 1989 when The FCFI Board named Bill Guindon to a newly created post of FCFI Liaison. As usual, Bill introduced himself in a "Meet a Member" column. Having grown up in and around the fire service in Astoria, OR, Bill finally joined the local fire department in 1985. Soon afterward he was caught in a conflagration, a blazing basement fire. He thought this might be the end, but the Lord saved him in more ways than one. As a result of that event Bill became a strong believer in the Lord Jesus Christ.

In 1987 he entered an intensive training program at Glen Eyrie. It was known as the Leadership Development Institute. This discipleship experience re-directed Bill's vision for his life. Although his first love was the fire service, he knew that he wanted to serve the Lord in some full-time capacity. During his time at Glen Eyrie Bill discovered the ministry of FCFI. In fact, he became vice president of the Pikes Peak chapter. [52]

His challenge was to visit as many chapters as possible. He set out to encourage the far-flung membership by actually sitting down with them in their firehouses. In the article announcing Bill's appointment, the purpose was put forward in simple terms: "He [Bill Guindon] believes the Lord is leading him to be a full-time missionary to the fire service." Bill would trust the Lord to provide for his needs, as he struck out to live by faith. [53]

By the next year, 1989, Bill logged more than 8,000 miles of travel and visited forty chapters. A picture of Bill and Dan Clegg, President of the Indianapolis chapter, illustrates this itinerant aspect of his ministry. *The Encourager* features frequent pictures of Bill with members all over the United States and also in Canada.

After two years of ministry the Board offered Bill an open-ended contract. An accompanying article in *The Encourager* explains that Bill needs to raise $2,000 per month for his living and travel expenses. Bill signed on for this challenge and continued his ministry. This enabled Bob Crum to give full effort to the headquarters in Denver. It also allowed Bob to remain home during the declining days of his wife, Doris.

In the spring of 1991 the Board issued a special message in *The Encourager*. Two years previously the Board had been asking the Lord for a full-time person to assist Bob Crum in the Denver office. Bill became the answer to that prayer. To quote the Board: "Bill has been a real work horse in getting information about FCF out to the public, to the fire service. Bill has done a great job of working with the chapters." [54]

Later that year Bill introduced his new wife, Pam. They had met as part of the Leadership Development Institute at Glen Eyrie. Pam had gone on to serve a short-term of ministry in Hong Kong. On July 13, 1991 she married Bill, and together they returned to the ministry of FCFI. Pam managed the office, while Bill continued to visit the chapters and spread the word.

During Bob Crum's last year as president, Pam became the editor of *The Encourager*. An unbroken series of editions bears witness to her faithfulness in this task. The format remains the same. It is a six-page format including the "Meet a Member," reports of various conferences and visits by Bill Guindon, and a steady flow of news from chapters across the country and around the world.

<u>A Time to Remember</u>

When America suffered its darkest day, on September 11, 2001, *The Encourager* chronicled the response of FCFI members and co-workers. From that time onward a FDNY (Fire Department of New York) insignia became part of the banner head. Next to this haunting symbol stand the words: "Let us never forget."

# Chapter 7

## Into All the World

"You are called to be an ambassador for Christ," (2 Cor. 5:20a) Bob Crum reminded the membership. Then he explained: "Being Christ's representative in all you do and say should be foremost in your life. You are called to be salt and light in the fire service. If you are going to have an impact on your fellow firefighters, a consistent, Godly testimony is critical." [55]

From the start FCFI was not just a club composed of firefighters. It was not designed to be a "Christian huddle," an exclusive fellowship oblivious to those outside its locked doors. Nor was it a "holy club," set up to coddle Christians. FCFI was designed from day one to be a light in the fire service. Its primary purpose was to draw men and women to Christ and encourage them in their walk with the Lord.

Almost fifteen years into the history of FCFI Bob Crum felt it necessary to remind the members of this call to communicate Christ. He urged readers of *The Encourager* to shine brightly for the Lord within the fire service. This has become a clear mark of the committed band of believers. From the earliest days firefighters reached out to brothers and sisters in the fire service, and they also undertook courageous and costly mission trips throughout America and around the world. This brief chapter will include only a few such exploits for Christ. Many others are reported in the pages of *The Encourager*, while others are known only to the Lord. Heaven will be their reward.

### Many Languages—Many Countries

Early in the history of FCFI we run into the name of Dr. Marie Berg. She undertook translating the literature of FCF into German, apparently her mother tongue. When we asked Bob Crum about this woman, he referred us to Duncan Wilkie. Duncan likewise had little information about the good doctor. She was a professor with a heart for the fire service, and Duncan recruited her to translate FCFI material into her native German language.

Others would take the news of FCFI as far as the Middle East and former Soviet Republics. A study of the newsletters reveals that Christian firefighters were able to penetrate countries that were otherwise closed to the cause of Christ.

### A Trumpeting Fire Captain

From Aurora, Illinois came the story of David Valentine. Dave was a training captain with the Aurora Fire Department. He had been converted in 1976 when he fell two and a half stories in a repelling accident. Due to the prayers of Christian friends he was back at work a short eight months after the accident.

He teamed up with a friend, Murray Clugston, to undertake missionary tours. Since Dave was a trumpet player, he joined in these overseas outreaches. Because Ukrainians hold firefighters in such high regard, Murray recruited Dave to join him in a missionary trip. Murray said: "This [connection to the fire service] would open doors for witnessing."

Dave asked Pam Guindon to lead the prayer charge: "Pray especially for God to speak through us, and allow my music to touch souls. Of course we won't 'turn down' prayers for travel connections and our safety on the trip." [56] Such short-term missionary outreaches had gained strength during the 1960s, and Dave Valentine capitalized on this exciting trend to lend his talents as a trumpet-playing fire captain to the newly opened country of the Ukraine.

### Belarus—Obscure but Open

The small, formerly Soviet republic of Belarus was largely uncharted territory. The official CIA *World Fact Book* contains this description of the Slavic nation: "After seven decades as a constituent republic of the USSR, Belarus attained its independence in 1991. It has retained closer political and economic ties to Russia than any of the other former Soviet republics. Belarus and Russia signed a treaty on a two-state union on the 8th of December 1999 envisioning greater political and economic integration. Although Belarus agreed to a framework to carry out the accord, serious implementation has yet to take place. Since his election in July 1994 as the country's first president, Aleksandr Lukashenko, has steadily consolidated his power through authoritarian means. Government restrictions on freedom of speech and the press, peaceful assembly, and religion remain in place." The capital is Minsk, and this small country is nestled between Lithuania, Latvia, and the Ukraine. [57]

In the October 1994 issue of *The Encourager* is a letter from Lyle Robinson, a professional and volunteer firefighter from Lacona, NY. In his straightforward style, Robinson writes: "The Lord has been moving in my heart for a long time with a burden for my fellow firefighters. In the last two weeks the Lord took my wife and me to Baranovichi, Belarus, part of the old Soviet Union. While I was there the Lord used me to share with the Fire Chief and other senior fire officers about Jesus and invite them to our service that night. The Lord used this to confirm to me my heart's desire to touch other firefighters with God's peace and love." [58]

### Saudi Crew Chief

Since time immemorial Saudi Arabia has been closed to Christian missionary activity. When the government discovered Christians in country, they were arrested, tortured, and very often slain for their faith. For these reasons, it is both amazing and encouraging to read the testimony of a firefighter from that ostensibly closed country.

"I have been a Christian for fourteen years and a firefighter for two of those years." Crew chief Kenneth Haase from King Abdulaziz International Airport Fire Department wrote to FCFI headquarters. Then he added: "Any information on your fellowship would be greatly appreciated."

Apparently this courageous Christian fire officer actually planned to affiliate with FCFI from his post at the international airport in Jeddah, Kingdom of Saudi Arabia. This serves to show the wide net spread by FCFI during its early years. Usually contact was made by advertisements inserted in widely read firefighter magazines.

There was no limit to the worldwide impact of FCFI. Everywhere Christian firefighters traveled they tied up with other firefighters. This led to contacts that literally encircled the globe on behalf of FCFI. But the same expansive witness characterized FCFI members here in the United States. Across America firefighters enlarged the reach of witness.

### Rick Barton on the Fire Line

As ambassador-at-large for FCFI Rick Barton is a true "renaissance man." He not only has distinguished seminary degrees, but he also has depth of experience in the fire service. His area of expertise is fighting wild fires across the United States. To gain an understanding of his life and work, we interviewed Rick. The following are his answers to the questions we posed:

*How did you make the first connection with Wildland firefighters?* I went on my first forest fire assignment in 1967 as a college student while working on a trail crew for the United States Forest Service. You might say I was "hooked" on Wildland fire fighting from that day on. My first dispatches were as part of Forest Service hand-crews; starting as a crewman, then squad boss and eventually crew boss. In the late 1980's I went into fire full-time as a fire engine foreman. Now I serve on Incident Management Teams as a Line Safety Officer, Public Information Officer, and Strike Team Leader. For a couple of years I organized a Type 2 hand crew called the "Maranatha Fire Crew" staffed with Christian college students.

In 1969 I gave my life to Jesus Christ. Initially, I was timid about sharing my faith on fire assignments but as the Holy Spirit continued to work in my life I became bolder. In 1987, the "Siege of 87" broke out in Northern California. Hundreds of crews responded to over 1000 new starts and I ended up as crew boss for a Forest Service hand crew.

We spent 28 days in heavy smoke, difficult terrain and extreme fire behavior. I became very lonely and desired for Christian fellowship. I realized there had to be other Christians on the line who felt the same. The next summer I began holding brief, interdenominational chapels on the fire line during lunch break or in camp after shift. I would yell out, "Hey guys, we're having church beside that rock and you're invited!" At almost every fire scene both men and women responded. What surprised me is that a number who weren't believers came, just to "check it out." They're more comfortable with a fellow firefighter doing the service than going to a "real" church.

After hearing about FCFI I ordered copies of *Answering the Call*, which was very well received. Christian and non-Christian alike pick up copies; first to read the stories and then God's word!

I have been privileged to give away several cases a year along with the "Firefighters and First Responders" devotional. Through working with structure fire resources on urban interface fires, I've been able to supply ATCs (*Answering the Call* New Testaments) and devotionals to many fire departments. We buy them and provide them at no charge. FCFI is an answer to prayer with resources, contacts, and *The Encourager* magazine. I try to be a voice for Wildland firefighters by writing articles and am encouraged to hear more and more Wildland firefighters are reading.

Wildland firefighters are called in to assist in a variety of "all risk" settings. As a result I've been able to hold chapels on the Space Shuttle Recovery, Hurricane Katrina response, and by candlelight during the Hurricane Ivan response. I was blessed to give 500 copies of the original FCFI New Testament to the New York Fire Department while serving in a respite center following 9/11.

*What are some of the most encouraging memories of that outreach?* There are many of course. I'll give you a few. One year, on a fire in Dinosaur National Monument, I announced the "church" service. Several came over to the rock and we began to pray and share the word. As I shared, I noticed one young man had slipped behind the other side of the rock and was listening in. I spoke a little louder and Jesus reached out and grabbed him!

During a large Yellowstone fire I announced a chapel to our crew. One fellow, a very obnoxious and coarse man, looked at me and said, "I bet you don't want me coming to your service." I almost answered, "You're right!", but instead told him I'd be honored if he did. He came.

One night as we were transitioning from a Colorado fire to a Wyoming one, I held a service in the hotel meeting room. A woman walked by and looked in. I invited her to join us. As she came in I recognized her as one I had prayed with on another fire. She shared later that she had backslid and was headed to the bar when we called out to her. She committed her life to Jesus that night and we put her in touch with other Christians in her district.

One day while I was speaking in Eastern Colorado, a woman approached me and said that her father-in-law was going to come hear me speak. She said he was the fire chief, hadn't been in church for over 40 years, had terminal cancer, and had committed adultery and was losing his family. The only reason he come to church was that I was a firefighter. The man came and over the next few months struggled with Christ. I was on a fire assignment in another part of the state when I received a call, he wanted to see me as soon as possible. I turned the engine over to my assistant and drove the hundred miles or so to see him. He gave his life to Jesus! Three days later he entered into glory! [59]

## Cycling Across America

Having responded to the Pentagon on 9/11, Craig Duck has a deep personal interest in this unique American tragedy. In order to commemorate the attacks, Craig recruited a crew to cycle across

America. He tells the story of this monumental task in the following paragraphs:

After the events of 9/11 several members of the District of Columbia Fire and EMS Department wanted to do something in honor of those who lost their lives. The decision was made to do a cross-country bicycle ride. Those in the department who helped to plan for the event decided it would be a good idea to end at the Pentagon at the exact time the plane had struck the building on September 11th. We would be doing this on the five-year anniversary of the tragic event. Some of the riders, including myself, were at the Pentagon that day and we felt like this would honor those who died there.

After much planning and advertising the small group was set to go. Tony Ferek and his wife Cindy, Ellen, and myself represented the Washington, D.C. Fire Department. We also had folks from the Baltimore Fire Department, and a small department in Kansas. Two other riders were not from fire departments, but wanted to ride to show their respect for firefighters. Along the way other bicycle riders who joined us for part of the trip. These new riders were always a blessing as it was new people to talk with.

Since I was a member of FCFInternational I wanted to make this a mission trip. After talking it over with Gay and Sue Reynolds, the President/Missionaries for FCFInternational, it was decided to use FCFInternational in order to get the word out to members. Several members gave financially, one big donation of 10 cases of *Answering the Call* Bibles came in, and many members prayed for our trip. Along the way it was truly a blessing to have the support of the members. It was a huge blessing when Gay and Sue drove to Monarch Pass, Colorado in order to meet with our group.

The group left San Francisco in August 1, 2006 on a bright sunny 82-degree day. We rode 90.77 miles and stopped at a firehouse in Sacramento, California. From there we averaged 100 miles a day staying mostly in firehouses. Since this was a mission trip we would always give a presentation to the firefighters. We would tell our stories of 9/11 and why we were doing this trip. We were able to give away all of our Bibles, literature about FCFInternational, and share the gospel with those who would listen. We were so blessed to have firehouses to stay in, with most places also providing a meal for us. In Eureka Kansas they held an event for us at the fairgrounds with most of the town coming out to see us. Even though I struggled that day on the bicycle, it was a blessing to be around those good folks from the heartland.

We met so many good folks along the way. On one stop in Gunnison, Colorado we meet an FCFInternational member by the name of Rick Barton. Everyone on the trip loved the old fashion cowboy style chuck wagon meal he and his department provided.

On another stop we met a chief of a little fire department named Bob. His four-man department was eager to talk with us. He was so proud to go and show us his first hydrant that he had put in his district; it was in the middle of nowhere. When I asked why he placed it there, he told me how a house was there at one point but burned down. He laughed when I asked him if he thought it was too late.

As we rode across country we saw a lot of God's marvelous creation. Most agreed that Utah was our favorite scenery. God has made some spectacular sites to enjoy, and they always look better from a bicycle. We climbed many mountains in the beginning and most of us loved the downhill portion after the tough climb up. My favorite downhill was Monarch Pass. I was able to go 51 MPH downhill. I must admit it is easy to get scared when going that fast. We were all a little jealous when we met a fellow cyclist who got pulled over by the police for going 62 MPH. I know I could never go that fast.

We handed out a lot of Bibles, prayed with a lot of folks, and worked hard at letting firefighters know about the love of God. I was blessed when Don Biggs showed up to help. With Don's arrival our trip really began to feel like a mission trip. Don was good at talking with other firefighters about his relationship with Christ. Many times we would pass Don when he found another firehouse that wasn't on our agenda and stopped in to see how they were doing, handing them a Bible as he left. Several times he was almost late to the next firehouse because he stayed and talked to firefighters about Christ.

We peddled our bicycles for 42 days and covered 3900 miles. One of the firefighters from DC who had been on several different cross country bicycle trips said that this was one of the better organized ones she had been on. I praise God that He was able to accomplish that, not me. God provided awesome weather for us. A heat wave had just crossed the country ahead of us and we enjoyed cooler than normal weather. God also provided dry conditions for us along the way. Of the 42 days we were on our bicycles we only encountered 2 hours of rain. Only God can do things like that. I will never forget the firefighter who didn't want any religious stuff because he liked to drink and do fun things with the fellows. I watched him as he left, he made sure none of his buddies were looking and then he took a Bible from our table. I am thankful that we were able to plant a seed that day. God will do the rest.

As planned, we ended at the Pentagon at the same exact time the plane had hit the building, five years to the date. We circled up in the parking lot that the truck company I worked on that day had parked in and we prayed. We prayed for the families that lost loved ones, we prayed for the firefighters who were affected by that day, and we prayed that God would continue to bless the nation and the fire service. I am thankful to God that He allowed me the opportunity to represent Him on this mission trip. We serve an awesome God who is able to do far more than we could ever want or ask. [60]

## Re-birthing a Fire Department

FCFI member Mike Whitby has shared in a remarkable outreach ministry. Together with members of his church in Vandalia, Ohio, he has helped to re-birth the Oneida County Volunteer Fire and Rescue Department in Kentucky. The following is an excerpt of Mike's thrilling report:

As the team neared Oneida with replacement fire vehicles, they were ordered to turn on all the lights, sirens, air horns, etc. a couple miles outside of town. They did just that and had themselves a little two-vehicle parade into town, and to the firehouse!

Many of the members of the fire department began to get quite anxious and began to want to call the dispatcher to inquire as to what was going on in case they missed a call, and mutual aid was coming into our territory due to hearing all the sirens and air horns.

The local leader, Mr. Gay, assured them that all was well, and that they should just wait and see what happens. About that time, the fire engine and rescue truck turned the corner and began to head up the street to the firehouse. The Oneida firefighters exclaimed: "Instantly, we saw OUR name on the side of a 'new' fire engine and ambulance."

The Vandalia, Ohio Sunday school class will never forget the day they changed an entire community's lives and their fire department forever, and neither will the Newstead Fire Co. members.

In the words of the recipients: "Tears of joy and gratitude filled the eyes of the Oneida Vol. Fire Dept. members and those of the citizens that we protect upon arrival of the two new vehicles and equipment."

The members of the Oneida Vol. Fire & Rescue Dept. stated over and over again that they never thought any one would ever help them. They thought they would never own any other fire engine. The one they had was in poor condition. The old fire engine was also one of the first mechanized fire engines to be purchased and used in Clay County, KY.

The Oneida Fire Department went under some major changes in 2006. In a nut shell, a brand new fire department was formed. Prior to 2006, OFD was run by extremely poor and crooked management. Oneida Vol. Fire & Rescue Dept. was a "family owned and operated" fire department so to speak. The former chief had an auto dealer's license. He would purchase vehicles under his name and the department name so that he could place them on department insurance policies. Our former chief purchased several department vehicles this way. He often fiddled with the insurance policies.

Finally, after much reporting, complaining, documentation, etc., the Common Wealth of Kentucky's Fire Commission stepped in and helped take the chief and family out of power. The Fire Commission declared the Oneida Vol. Fire & Rescue Department non-existent. It gave the department a list of things that had to be accomplished, documented, and so on before it could be recognized as a fire department in the Common Wealth of Kentucky again. The Fire Commission went as far as to issue a new fire department state identification number, and revoked the old one. [61] All this occurred because concerned Christian brothers in Ohio reached out to help a needy fire department in Kentucky.

# Chapter 8

## Spreading the Word—Chapters Come to Life

Touch the life of a local chapter, and you get your fingers on the pulse of FCFI. Across the country firefighters meet together regularly to pray for each other, share learned lessons from God's Word, and strategize ways to help other firefighters.

Late in 2012 a "Meet A Member" column featured Rob Kloss from the West Grove Fire Company in Landenberg, PA. As a young man, Rob is something of a newcomer to FCFI, but his story resonates with all of us. Here is how he expressed it:

"In 2008 I finally acted on the dream of becoming a firefighter. I am a volunteer for the West Grove Fire Company in Pennsylvania and have loved the learning and the challenges inherent to it. I formed a chapter [of FCFI] here in Chester County in the hope that God will use it as a vehicle to glorify Himself through it.

"My prayer is that other responders would be drawn to attend and perhaps come to find the truth. I pray that they will find out that there is only one way to fill that void that [Blaise] Pascal talked about, to discover that peace which is beyond all understanding. My heart breaks for those who don't know Him. I don't know in what ways the Lord is moving, but I pray He'll use us to bring others to Him in whatever ways He deems fit."

He refers to Blaise Pascall (1623-62), who was a French mathematician, philosopher, and Christian thinker. He spoke of an "infinite abyss" in the human heart, which can be filled only by an "infinite and immutable object; in other words, by God Himself." [62]

It is unusual for a firefighter to quote Blaise Pascal, but the newest generation of firefighters are some of the best-educated in the history of America's fire service. Rob is symbolic of that generation.

However, we remind ourselves that the present generation of young firefighters stands on the shoulders of giants. The same is true of FCFI. The present generation of firefighters are erecting a spiritual superstructure within the fire service, and the basis is with our FCFI founding generation. Many of their chapters still persist, and we will look at some of these chapters in the present section of this little history.

### A Capital Idea—Washington, D.C. Chapter

Our new President/Missionary Lt. Craig Duck represents the Washington, D.C. chapter. He commented on it in the "Meet A Member" column that introduced Craig and his wife, Holly.

Craig joined the D.C. Fire Department in January 1986. Immediately before taking up this appointment, Craig became a believer in the Lord Jesus Christ. Shortly thereafter Craig and Holly married, and together they began life in the Nation's Capital. Craig recalls that this was an exciting time in his life as God began to shape him into the man God planned and purposed. God would make him a "vessel to be used for His honor and glory."

Craig continues the story: "God led me to a small group of firefighters that loved the Lord and met together for fellowship and Bible study. What a joy to learn that God was using the Fellowship of Christian Firefighters in similar firehouses all across America and around the world.

"It was in this local chapter that Don Biggs shared with us the importance of being a worthy testimony in the fire service, something that seemed to come natural to him. It was in that small group where I learned about Gay and Sue Reynolds and the entire ministry that FCFInternational was involved in."

In the same article, Craig Duck paints a big picture for FCFI. He reminds us that there are 1.1 million firefighters in the United States, and that they serve in 51,300 firehouses. To continue this big picture, Craig adds: "Every day in America 66,800 pumpers, 6,800 aerial apparatus, 72,800 other suppression vehicles, and who knows how many ambulances are running up and down the street."

He challenges us by saying: "The Bible encourages us, 'therefore pray earnestly to the Lord of the harvest to send out laborers into his harvest' (Matt. 9:38 ESV)." Then he adds: "You can be salt and light in the fire service." [63]

Notice one name in Craig's article. It is Don Biggs. Don summarized his experience in the District of Columbia in this insightful interview:

*How did you first come into contact with FCFI?* Kenny Cox was in the DC Department a year or so before I joined. He was assigned to Ladder Truck 10, and I was assigned to Engine 13 in the same house in January 1967. All the time I have known him he has been a Christian. We used to talk and he invited me to their church a few times. Kenny was, and still is very outgoing.

He told me on a number of occasions that when he would go to the IAFF Conventions he had a group of Firefighters that would seek out a restaurant where there was no smoking or drinking so they could have a pleasant meal together and talk about Christian stuff. Sounds almost like a FCFI meeting, but it all goes back a number of years before FCFI actually had its beginning. We can usually look back and see the hand of God working in people's lives. In this case God prepared us to be ready when the leadership came along by way of Duncan Willkie, Bob Crum, John Barker. They stepped out in faith to start a much-needed Christian Fellowship in the fire service. The idea was simple: Christian Firefighters, some in the same station, or same department, could be in contact with others around the country and around the world.

I believe Kenny told me about an article in a fire department publication concerning the FCFI. I'm not really sure at what date I joined FCFI. It seems to have been before 1982. I also have some t-shirts that we got in 2007 that say we have been coming to the mountain for 25 years. That's the Eastern Family Conference. Our Kids use to say if we cannot go anywhere else during the year we want to go to the Family Conference. They have made some lifelong friends there and they had freedom to get out and have their own classes geared to their ages. When we first went there we camped for a number of years, and then moved to higher ground.

One other thing, early on I can remember that David, my son and I went to Emmetsburg, the Fire Academy and picked up Duncan Willkie and brought him back to the DC area, but for the life of me I don't remember what we did with him after we got back. Maybe he would remember.

*When and where did you start the chapter?* So, it looks as if the chapter in Washington, D.C. began prior to, or about 1982. This is only five years after the formal organization of FCFI in Denver. By 1982 I sent an FCFI Bible to Keith Helms of the Charlotte Fire Department.

*What is the greatest blessing you have experienced in this ministry?* It is like it happened yesterday. Our chapter had been going for a while. Kenny Cox was well on his way in the work of the fire department union. This still brings a tear to my eyes when I think about it. A fireman named Frank Palumbo from a ladder truck in New York City was the treasurer of the IAFF. It was election time, and Frank knew he had enough votes to be re-elected, but when the votes were counted he had lost the election. He was devastated and was pretty much wiped out. He had had a long standing in the IAFF and had moved to Vienna, VA to work at the headquarters of IAFF, which is in Washington, D.C.

Kenny knew Frank very well and I believe that he led him to the Lord. A short time later Kenny brought Frank to one of our FCFI meetings. We prayed with him and he told us his story. As I said above you can look back and see the hand of God working things out to get Frank into His service. Frank and his wife were Catholics, but I remember God had His hand on Frank. Frank blossomed, since I lived in a line between Frank and DC, he would come to our home and we would ride together to the meetings. After the meeting we would have fellowship together at our home, sometimes for hours. Frank found a church in Montgomery County, MD. He taught Sunday School there and went on several mission trips to Romania. He had opportunities to connect with Catholics.

Another memory is when Josie was bleeding internally and passed out at home. I called 911, the paramedics worked on her for a while. All the time David stood by watching every move they made. I believe that's when he decided to become a Firefighter/Paramedic later on. Anyway when we got to the hospital I was waiting in the waiting room praying to God to heal her. There was a phone there. I called Mark West our vice-president at the time and I knew he was supposed to be working. He prayed with me over the phone and a peace came over me that only God could put there. It relaxed me to the point that I knew the Lord had everything under control. Josie got better and healed.

*Why is FCFI important for the fire service?* It all boils down to believing and practicing what Hebrews 10:25 says and means about encouraging one another. Encouragement has always been the byword of FCFI internationally, nationally, and locally. Even though I am retired now, I can still have fellowship with firefighters here in Charlotte, NC. [64]

### Reaching New Jersey

As Director for New Jersey and Metropolitan New York, Russ Stammer has unstintingly given of himself to launch chapters of FCFI. He tells the following story: "I found a Bible placed by the FCFI in my firehouse. I had been praying about a Christian firefighter group but had no idea how to put one together. The Bible was old and the contact information was no longer valid, so I did not know if the FCFI still existed. I was attending the NJ State Firemen's Convention and found a listing of books of which one was *Sirens For The Cross,* and the description said the author was a regional director for the FCFI. I called directory assistance and got Tommy Neiman's number and called him. That is how I got in touch with the FCFI.

Then Russ adds detail about the first New Jersey chapter: "The first chapter I founded was in Oakland, New Jersey in 2000." Since then he has been an extremely active regional director for FCFI in the Metropolitan New York and New Jersey areas.

When asked about God's working in his area, Russ responds with this ringing testimony: "The greatest blessing in my FCFI ministry have been the friends I have made in the fire service across the country as well as those I have been able help because of my faith, that I might not have been able to help if it were not for being involved in the FCFI."

Russ knows how to put the ministry of FCFI into perspective for the entire fire service. He remarks: "The men and women of the fire service are searching. In fires they know what they are searching for, but in life many do not know what it is that they are looking for. The membership of the FCFI can help these people find the Lord who will provide everything they are missing in their lives." [65]

<u>The Heartland of America—Indianapolis</u>

From the first Dan Clegg has been a part of the Indianapolis chapter. He helped to launch it and thirty years later he is still part of that fellowship. Some of Dan's memories are recorded to describe the sage of FCFI in Indianapolis. Here are Dan's own words:

Indianapolis Fellowship of Firefighters was founded in 1972. We began our organization with five members: Lt. Morris Miller, Engineer Joe Bosslyn, Bob Rice, Tom Long and myself. This organization was meeting on a monthly basis with back-to-back days to accommodate the three-shift system. We began our meetings at the Thompson Road Baptist Church in Indianapolis. Lt. Miller served as our president, we continued in this for about three years. At that time four of the five of us felt that it was not working so we lay dormant for about five years.

After that time, I began to receive phone calls from two main people: Lt. Jack White and Engineer Don Presley. Because they were interested in reorganizing, I put out a notice for our reorganizational meeting. At that meeting I was put into the presidency of the new organization. I served in that capacity for about five years, and our numbers grew from the five original members. I was the only one of the first five involved in the reorganization. Bob Rice and Maury Miller have gone home to be with Jesus since this date. Tom Long, Joe Bosslyn and myself are retired.

When I left the presidency Lieutenant Jack White took over that position. I acted in the position of chaplain to the fellowship. During this stage of the fellowship we tried various meeting places, restaurants, fire stations, individuals' homes, as well as churches.

Jack served as our president until 1999. At which point I took over the position once again. I remained in that position serving as both President and Chaplain. During that time our numbers grew. At the time of my retirement in 2001 I had approximately 125 names on the roster, who would have claimed to be a part of us. Many of them never attended meetings or joined FCFInternational.

I tried to hold down the presidency for about two years after my retirement. Without having access to the watch room via the computer I found it difficult to do. At which time as regional director I appointed Gilbert Gaddie to take over as president of the Indianapolis chapter. Gilbert did an excellent job for a number of years before he began having some health problems due to line of duty injuries he had while with IFD. In 2011, Gilbert stepped away from that position.

When our organization began in 1972, we were referred to by

a lot of different names: the God squad, religious fanatics, even Jesus freaks. Since that time we have seen a lot of changes. We were given permission to place Bibles in all fire stations; we served on committees to help find a new Fire Chaplain for IFD. They have placed our name in the five history books of IFD. We have been asked to serve on several committees. We are allowed to be in all orientations of the new firefighters coming on the job for the past 25 years. We present all recruits with the New Testament Bibles [*Answering The Call*]. With the help of the Firefighters Credit Union we were also able to purchase 200 copies of Tommy Neiman's book, *Sirens For The Cross* to place in all Marion County firehouses. We gave a copy to all Indianapolis Fire Department retirees at that time as a Christmas gift.

We have also been allowed to do an article in the *Helmet*, which is our union monthly newsletter. At one point in time we used the Union hall as a meeting place and for a short period of time we were allowed to place materials at the union hall, for fund-raising purposes. The union also allowed us to place the "Firefighters Prayer" at the memorial outside of the union hall for fallen firefighters.

It has been a blessing serving as a member of the Fellowship of Christian Firefighters and I have seen God work in many different ways. I can tell you about situations where I have been able to witness on the fire scenes. I can also give you situations where I was awarded a certificate of appreciation for doing the job of the Chaplain when no other one was available.

We responded on first aid runs, we fought fires, and I served as a chaplain all on the same runs. In my last assignment as engineer on engine 18 my captain came to me, took my report book, and told me to do the job that I did best as a Chaplain. This happened on at number of locations. When we began the fellowship there was many who mocked us. But God turned it to His glory.

NOTE: Dan Clegg is one of the jewels in the history of FCFI. For more than thirty years he has lived out a consistent witness for Christ in and around the Indianapolis Fire Department. His modest report reveals only the briefest outlines of his ministry with and through the members of the Indianapolis Fire Department. His role as a regional director of FCFI has served to perpetuate that ministry, and as a result several generations of firefighters have heard a credible, powerful presentation of the gospel. As Dan says, "But God turned it to His glory!" [66]

## Bible Belt Firefighters

By most standards, Charlotte, North Carolina is the "buckle on the Bible Belt." The long-time Chapter president of FCFI in Charlotte is retired Battalion Chief Keith Helms. He shares with us the story of FCFI in Charlotte. The following are Keith's answers to our questions about chapter life:

*How did you first come into contact with FCF?* I became a believer in Jan. of 1980. Two years later I joined the Charlotte Fire Department. My wife and I were attending Calvary Church in Charlotte, and our elder was Phil Devine. Phil's brother–in-law was Don Biggs, an engineer in the Washington, D.C. Fire Department. Don was a member of the Fellowship of Christian Firefighters and he gave an FCFI Station Bible to Phil, which was then delivered to me. The Bible had an insert with information on FCFI, and this enabled us to contact the organization.

*When and where did you start your chapter?* In 1982, after receiving the information on the ministry, several firefighters began to meet for Bible study and fellowship. The informal meetings continued to grow for the next year. In November, 1983, we officially formed the Charlotte-Mecklenburg chapter of the Fellowship of Christian Firefighters.

*What is the greatest blessing you have experienced in this ministry?* I have been blessed in many ways through this ministry. I have been encouraged by other brothers and have been mentored by FCFI members such as Wayne Detzler. The greatest blessing is the opportunity to serve firefighters and their families in a manner that glorifies the Lord.

Largely because of the recommendation of FCFI, Wayne Detzler became chaplain of the Charlotte Fire Department. He served there until his retirement at the end of 2006, at which time he was member of a thriving chapter of FCFI and dynamic team of peer chaplains.

*Why is FCFI important for the fire service?* "The fire service is a mission field. Unbelieving firefighters need a saving relationship with God through faith in Christ. Believing firefighters need to grow in grace and in the knowledge of our Lord and Savior. FCFI is a ministry that encourages firefighters to actively minister in this field. FCFI aims to evangelize the unbelievers and to equip and empower the believers. Firefighters face many harsh difficulties in this life. FCFI points struggling firefighters to Christ." [67]

### Treasure Coast (FL) Chapter

Lt. Tommy Neiman is part of the FCFI team in Florida. He retold the story of his connection with FCFI in a recent email. Tommy came into contact with FCFI in 1986 when Bob Crum visited the area and met our then Fire Chaplain Jack Favorite. This was fairly early on in the history of FCFI, and Bob was busy multiplying contacts and chapters across the United States.

When asked about the founding of the first chapter in Florida's Treasure Coast, Neiman responded: "We founded our first chapter here St. Lucie County Fire Rescue [Treasure Coast chapter] back in the summer of 1986." Here again it was one responder moved by the call of Christ to launch a chapter in a new place.

"The greatest blessing is seeing firefighters come to know Christ." Evangelism is the heartthrob of FCFI, and there is a strong sense of mission. FCFI members across the land see their role as missionaries within the fire service and among the first responder community.

When asked why FCFI is important to the fire service, Tommy Neiman responded with the following sentence: "FCFI is important to fire service because it gives believing firefighters an organization to belong to as Christians in the fire service."

In 1998 Tommy Neiman published his popular book, *Sirens for the Cross*. Since then he has collaborated with Sue Reynolds to produce several editions of this valuable evangelistic tool. Tommy continues to serve as a firefighter/paramedic with the St. Lucie Fire District in Ft. Pierce. In 2003 he was honored as "Firefighter of the Year" for the state of Florida.

# Chapter 9

## The Darkest Day

By any standards, September 11, 2001 stands out in the memory of all of America's first responders as "the darkest day." The enormous toll of death and destruction in New York, Washington, and even rural Pennsylvania defies our comprehension. To help us understand we are including the testimonies of FCFI members who saw it all first hand. Many of their testimonies are included in the devotional book edited by Gay and Sue Reynolds, *Stories of Faith and Courage from Firefighters and First Responders.* [68]

"The Pentagon was the largest disaster any of us had ever responded to," Craig Duck remembers. He explains: "The radio was abuzz with priority messages… firefighters trying to explain what they needed. The scene was chaos." When the chief arrived on scene things began to change. The attack on the fire became organized. Firefighters calmed down to combat the blazes." [69]

<u>In New York—The Towers Fell</u>

Joe Smaha tries to comprehend the scene in lower Manhattan, as the World Trade Center towers tumbled into a heap of ash. The Paramas, NJ Haz-Mat team was deployed to back up FDNY Haz-Mat number one. Joe Smaha arrived on scene to the Paramas squad. He remembers first impressions. First, the disaster area was enormous, sixteen acres. Second, everywhere were the sickening signs of lost human life. Broken bodies and bits of bodies littered the scene. Third, an eerie stillness hovered over the entire scene. There was no pedestrian traffic at all. The only sound was the wailing sirens as they sped to the gaping scar in the skyline.

<u>Comfort for the Grieving</u>

The attacks of 9/11 enabled FCFI to do what it does best. Its task was the comfort of survivors. But how do you get your arms around a city in grief, a nation in mourning? The initial response was a Blue and White service, as the mourning began. FCFI members responded by offering memorial flags and ornamental urns to the families of victims.

Tommy Neiman remembers those first days: "As each family came forward, I experienced sadness and a powerful desire to comfort them. So deep was their loss, many had to be held up as they received their urn." [70] It reminds us of the biblical instruction, "weep with them that weep." (Rom. 12:15)

Tommy also helps to put the devastation of 9/11 into perspective, especially for first responders: "To many, it is not *Ground Zero*, but...*Ground Hero*, for on those New York City grounds, where the stately 110-story World Trade Center towers once stood, many of America's true heroes gave their lives." Tommy saw it first hand, when he visited recovery teams and prayed with and for them. [71]

In his role as leader of FCFI Gay Reynolds organized the response to 9/11. While preparing for this book, we asked Gay to reflect on his experience in New York following the attacks of 9/11. The following is his response:

September 11, 2001, our nation was in shock. We'd been attacked. The FCFI phone rang constantly. 'How can I help?' and 'What role will FCFI play in this tragedy?' The outpouring of love and concern was a tribute to the heart of FCFI's members. We had folks in place to help where needed. Unfortunately, government restrictions were many, but we serve a great God and He opened the door for me to represent FCFI on two trips to New York City, one while Sue held down the FCFI office and another when she accompanied me.

The second trip began on Tuesday, October 23. We hurriedly finished the November/December issue of *The Encourager*, packed, and headed east. News of discouragement setting in reached our ears. Rescue had a new face and name: Recovery. In addition, The North Jersey chapter president, Russ Stammer, and vice president, Reverend Joe Smaha, felt that the doors for ministry were beginning to open in New York City. Two and half days and 1750 miles later, we arrived in New Jersey in time for the North Jersey chapter meeting.

These brothers had been directly impacted by the Attack on America. FCFI member, Gary Pederson, shared the Memorial Program from the services of one of his co-workers. In the middle of the program was a picture of the three children and wife of this fallen brother. The tragedy took a more personal form as we witnessed the pain etched in Gary's face. Joe Smaha shared how his faith sustained him through his days as part of the Haz-Mat team stationed at Ground

Zero immediately after the Attack, as well during his personal contacts with families of victims in the aftermath.

During the meeting I received a call from the New York Office of Emergency Management asking if I could arrange for a group of FCFI chaplains and pastors to pass out ceremonial urns to the families of victims the following Sunday in Liberty Park. In lieu of a body, loved ones would at least have an urn with dust from where their loved one gave his or her life. Isn't God great? We were in the area and I was able to say, 'We'd be blessed to do that.'

Sunday proved to be a busy day. At 7:00 a.m. Florida regional director, Tommy Neiman, who flew in to assist with the services, joined Russ, Joe, and me in an interview by Juke Box Radio 103.1 FM out of Dumont, NJ. We were given the opportunity to share FCFI and most importantly the Lord. Then we were off to a special Blue and White Service at Community Alliance Church to honor emergency personnel. An uplifting service and time of fellowship and food followed.

Then seven FCFI fire chaplains, Russ Stammer, Joe Smaha, Tommy Neiman, Dave Hutsebault, Bill Williamsen, Dennis Seeley, and I headed for Liberty Island. At 2:00 p.m. a memorial service was held. For the first time since the Attack, all work at "Ground Zero" ceased for twenty-four hours to allow families of victims to gather, pray, and see the results of the tragedy that took their loved one. After the televised service, families were taken to Liberty Island for a private service and presentation.

Thousands of people—families of those lost in the rubble of the World Trade Center—gathered behind private walls of a tent in Liberty Island to receive urns and flags: Flags for our country's heroes, dust from the pulverized buildings that claimed so many lives.

There are no adequate words to share the blessings we received from being able to present the victim's families with these mementoes. I went to help, serve, and bless, but I was the one blessed. Love was everywhere in the midst of sorrow. People came to us and asked for prayer. People thanked us for being there. God opened the door, we walked through it, and we were able to share and reflect God's love. It was incredible.

Following the presentation, the opportunity opened for us to pray with many other people and visit several stations before being escorted into 'Ground Zero.' At one station (The Ten Ten House), eight people prayed to receive Christ as their Savior. Over one hundred FCFI *Bibles* and *Sirens For The Cross* books were given out at stations and throughout the area. (More continue to be handed out to this day along with devotionals). If ever a person doubts the goodness and love of people, a trip to 'Ground Zero,' where hatred ruled for only a few moments, would allay those doubts.

The network of the Fellowship of Christian Firefighters proved a blessing once again when George Rabiela, was then the Chicago FCFI regional director, recommended we look up Reverend Bob Ossler, who was serving his third stint at St. Paul's Episcopal Church. Joe Smaha, Russ Stammer, Sue, and I traveled the maze-like, smoke-filled, eerily abandoned streets around the once towering WTC in route to 'Ground Zero.' When we arrived we were escorted past tables filled with candy bars, soft drinks, water, coffee, (all manned by volunteers) and into the church. The pews were lined with thousands of notes from thankful citizens nationwide—some obviously penned at the hand of children, others from adults. Rev. Bob was praying with two volunteers but immediately joined us at the end of the prayer with hugs and appreciation. He had been praying and counseling people around the clock and had performed nearly 300 memorial or funeral services on the mound. Now God provided us with the privilege of praying for and with our fellow brother and FCFI member, Bob.

Many other members played an active role in the aftermath of 9/11 helping in rescue, clean up, ministry, and reflecting God's love.

# Chapter 10

## Craig Duck—Facing Forward

As we enter the year 2013, Lieutenant Craig Duck of the Washington, D.C. Fire Department becomes President/Missionary of the Fellowship of Christian Firefighters International. Craig's powerful personal testimony will introduce him, and his vision for our fellowship will conclude this book.

"Share your testimony," we asked Craig to bring us up-to-date in his life and family. He graciously responded with the following:

Every Saturday when I was a child, my dad took me to the firehouse in upstate New York. My mom still loves showing the picture of me when I was about five years old sitting proudly on the fire truck my dad drove in a parade. I can't remember a time when I didn't want to be a firefighter.

When I graduated from high school I headed to New York City to attend John Jay College for fire administration. I hoped that by attending college in New York City I could become a firefighter for FDNY. I read every book and article I could find about FDNY. I thought they were the best of the best and I wanted to be a part of that department.

I soon discovered that New York City isn't a good place to attend college when you're a young impressionable firefighter from a small town. I was easily influenced, most of the time for all the wrong reasons. Some of the New York City firefighters I hung out with loved to drink alcohol. Wanting to impress them, I fell into the same sin. Soon my grades began to drop and I struggled with who I was and why I was on earth. I was not attending church regularly and I had no idea what my purpose in life was.

During one of my breaks from college I went home to Syracuse, New York. The volunteer department in Syracuse, where I was still a member, was having their annual installation banquet. I needed a date and a good friend of mine knew a nice girl, named Holly, who wanted to attend the banquet. Why she was willing to go with me is still mind boggling, but I'm thankful she did.

After the banquet I met her dad, Glenn. During one of our conversations, he shared the plan of salvation. I'd never heard that God loved me and wanted to have a personal relationship with me. After sharing God's love, Glenn looked directly at me and asked, 'If you were to die in a fire tonight, where would you spend eternity?' Wow. I didn't know where I would spend eternity, and I could not get that picture out of my mind. Glenn then shared with me the plan of salvation.

After much thought and a subsequent Sunday sermon by Pastor Saucer, I prayed and asked God to forgive me of my sins. I asked Jesus Christ to be the Lord of my life and I determined to follow Him all of my life. Since then God has never let me down. That was 29 years ago. That nice girl, Holly, is now my wife and we have 4 sons. I finished fire school, and have served the Lord faithfully as a firefighter for 28 years as a part of the District of Columbia Fire and EMS Department. In 2012 after much prayer God opened the door for Holy and I to serve as the President and Missionaries for FCFInternational."

## How About You

If you were to die tonight in an emergency, where would you spend eternity?

The plan Glenn shared with me many years ago has never changed and it is God's plan for everyone who is willing to make that choice. God has prepared a wonderful place called heaven. Scripture clearly explains that in heaven "God shall wipe away all tears from their eyes; and there shall be no more death, neither sorrow, nor crying, neither shall there be any more pain: for the former things are passed away." (Revelation 21:4)

The Bible also tells us that heaven is a beautiful place. The only problem is that because of sin we cannot get to heaven on our own good deeds. The Bible says in Romans that "For all have sinned, and come short of the glory of God" (Romans 3:23). Not only are we sinners but the Bible goes on to explain; "For the wages of sin is death; but the gift of God is eternal life through Jesus Christ our Lord." (Romans 6:23)

How exciting to find out that God has provided a free gift to anyone who believes. "For God so loved the world, that he gave his only begotten Son, that whosoever believeth in him should not perish, but have everlasting life." (John 3:16)

So what is causing you not to pray to God in order to confess your sins? What would stop you from calling out to God right now? The Bible encourages us "That if thou shalt confess with thy mouth the Lord Jesus, and shalt believe in thine heart that God hath raised him from the dead, thou shalt be saved." (Romans 10:9)

If you prayed to ask Jesus Christ to forgive you of your sins and to become Lord of your life, please let the International Office know (Information on the back cover). It would truly be a blessing and we would love to send you some resources to help you in your walk with Christ.

Recently the vision statement has been changed in order to more accurately reflect some of the core values of FCFInternational. Our vision is to glorify God in the fire service by building relationships that turn first responders hearts and minds toward Jesus Christ (Philippians 2:11) and to equip them to serve Him (Ephesians 4:12). Our prayer is that members will build relationships with other first responders in the places God has placed them. FCFInternational wants to be able to equip members to fulfill Matthew 28:19 & 20 in regards to making disciples in the fire service. FCFInternational looks forward to the day when God will call many first responders to Himself through our discipleship ministry.

The mission of FCFInternational is to encourage one another to share the vision with the fire service community through

**W**itnessing, **P**raying, **T**eaching the Word, and **W**alking worthy. Utilizing prayer and the discipleship ministry FCFInternational hopes to reach the 1.2 million firefighters in the United States as well as the untold number in other countries. We look forward to the day when FCFInternational members are sought after for promotion and encouraged to join certain departments because of their testimony for God. Our prayer continues to be that we will find local chapters in each of the 50 states and every country in the world. The International Office will continue to tirelessly work in order to develop resources that can be placed in first responders hands that will help them to have a meaningful relationship with God.

While we have been given a good foundation from our founders, there remains a lot of work to be done. This ministry of God's is too big and too difficult for one individual. Our prayer is that many members would pray about their involvement in FCFInternational. As more and more members catch the vision and strive to fulfill the mission of FCFInternational in their local departments I am confident that we will see real changes in the fire service. Revivals begin when the people of God get serious about serving Him and obeying the truths found in the Bible. Through the years we have seen many faithful members of FCFInternational serving God. I look forward to see what this generation can do to advance the kingdom of God. My prayer is to echo the words of Chris Tomlin in his song *Give us Clean Hands*; "Oh God let this be a generation who seeks, who seeks Your face, oh God of Jacob". May

God continue to bless you as you daily walk with Him and may God continue to bless the Fellowship of Christian Firefighters International.

# NOTES

1         Duncan Wilkie, "Letter from the President," *The Encourager*, 1/1 (Feb.-Mar. 1978) 1, 3.
2         Bob Crum, "From the Secretary," *The Encourager*, 1/1 (Feb.-Mar. 1978) 1-2
3         John Barker, Email response, May 17, 2012.
4         Duncan Wilkie, "President's Letter," The Encourager, 3/5 (Sept.-Oct. 1980) 1-2.
5         Bob Crum, "From the Desk of the Secretary," *The Encourager*, 3/3 (May-June 1980), 1, 6.
6         John Barker, "Meet A Member," *The Encourager*, 6/3 (May-June 1983) 1, 6.
7         Duncan Wilkie, "Looking into God's Word: PRAYER—Format and Faith," The Encourager,
          3/1 (Jan.-Feb. 1980), 2.
8         "1981 Family Conference Echoes—Snow Mountain Ranch," *The Encourager*
          4/4 (July-Aug. 1981), 5-6.
9         "Meet a Member," *The Encourager*, 3/1 (Jan.-Feb. 1980), 1, 3.
10        "Meet a Member," *The Encourager*, 4/2 (Mar.-Apr.1981), 1, 5.
11        "Meet a Member," *The Encourager*, 5/1 (Jan.-Feb. 1982), 1, 5.
12        *The Encourager*, 3/1 (Jan.-Feb., 1980), 4
13        *The Encourager*, 3/1 (Jan.-Feb. 1980), 4
14        *The Encourager*, 3/3 (May-June 1980), 2.
15        The Fellowship story began in 1961 with the formation of the Glasgow Fire Brigade and Glasgow
          Salvage Corps Christian Fellowship. This is believed to be the first established Christian Fellowship in the British Fire Services, although there has been London City Missionaries working amongst London Firefighters since 1845 and over the years there has been a small number of isolated Christian groups in County and Metropolitan Fire Brigades. http://firefightersforchrist.co.uk. Accessed Oct. 19, 2012.
16        "President's Praises," *The Encourager* , 8/6 (Nov.-Dec. 1985), 4
17        *The Encourager*, 11/2 (May-June 1988), 4.
18        *The Encourager*, 11/6 (Nov.-Dec. 1988), 3.
19        *The Encourager*, 13/3 (May-June 1990), 1.
20        *The Encourager*, 13/3 (May-June 1990), 5.
21        *The Encourager*, 15/5 (Nov.-Dec. 1992), 3.
22        *The Encourager*, 13/2 (Mar.-Apr. 1990), 5.
23        *The Encourager*, 8/4 (July-Aug. 1985), 4.
24        *The Encourager*, 12/5 (Nov.-Dec. 1989), 5.
25        *The Encourager*, 15/5 (Nov.-Dec. 1992), 7.
26        *The Encourager*, 16/4 (July-Aug. 1993), 4.

27  Bill Guindon, email response, Oct. 31, 2012.
28  Bill Guindon, email response, Oct. 31, 2012.
29  *The Encourager*, 16/5 (Sept.-Oct. 1993), 3.
30  Steve Seltzner, personal letter, April 15, 1994.
31  *The Encourager*, 17/6 (Oct.-Nov. 1994), 3.
32  *The Encourager*, 17/5 (Aug.-Sept. 1994), 3.
33  *The Encourager*, 15/3 (May-June 1992), 3.
34  *The Encourager*, 16/4 (July-Aug. 19930, 3.
35  *The Encourager,* 17/5 (Aug.-Sept. 1994), 3.
36  Randy Patterson, personal letter, Sept. 14, 1993.
37  *The Encourager*, 15/1 (Jan.-Feb. 1992), 5.
38  *The Encourager,* 15/1 (Jan.-Feb. 1992), 5.
39  Steve Bohannan, personal letter, Oct. 24, 1992.
40  Mark Stefanski. Undated personal letter.
41  *The Encourager*, 17/6 (Oct.-Nov. 1994), 3.
42  *The Encourager*, 16/3 (May-June 1993), 5.
43  Bill Guindon, email response, Oct. 31, 2012.
44  *The Encourager*, 1/1 (Feb.-Mar. 1978), 1.
45  *The Encourager*, 13/3 (May-June 1990), 1.
46  *The Encourager*, 12/1 (Jan.-Feb. 1989), 1.
47  *The Encourager*, 11/5 (Sept.-Oct. 1988), 5.
48  *The Encourager*, 1/2 (Apr.-May 1978), 1.
49  *The Encourager*, 11/1 (Jan.-Feb. 1988), 1.
50  *The Encourager*, 14/6 (Jan.-Feb., 1991), 1.
51  *The Encourager*, 15/1 (Jan.-Feb. 1992), 1.
52  *The Encourager*, 11/6 (Nov.-Dec. 1988), 1.
53  *The Encourager*, 11/6 (Nov.-Dec. 1988), 4.
54  *The Encourager*, 14/3 (May-June 1991).
55  *The Encourager*, 14/5 (Sept.-Oct. 1991), 5.
56  David Valentine, Letter to Pam Guindon, Jan. 28, 1993.
57  https://www.cia.gov/library/publications/the-world-factbook, accessed Nov. 14, 2012.
58  *The Encourager*, 17/6 (Oct.-Nov. 1994), 3.
59  Rick Barton, email interview, Nov. 10, 2012.
60  Craig Duck, email interview, Nov. 11, 2012.
61  Michael Whitby, "The History of The Oneida Vol. Fire & Rescue Dept. Re-Organization Effort," Nov. 16, 2012.
62  "Meet a Member," *The Encourager*, 35/5 (Sept.-Oct. 2012), 1-2.

63   "Meet a Member," *The Encourager*, 35/6 (Nov.-Dec. 2012), 1-2.
64   Dolph Biggs, email inter view, Nov. 20, 2012.
65   Russell Stammer, email interview, Nov. 13, 2012.
66   Dan Clegg, email interview, Oct. 26, 2012.
67   Keith Helms, email interview, Nov. 13, 2012.
68   G. and S. Reynolds, *Stories of Faith and Courage from Firefighters and First Responders*
     (Chattanooga: God and Country Press, 2010).
69   Ibid., 336-7.
70   Ibid., 342.
71   Ibid., 345.

Made in United States
North Haven, CT
08 May 2025